THE PRACTICAL ENCYCLOPEDIA OF

WHOLE FOODS

excretion, and also helps to reduce blood cholesterol. Both types of fibre reduce the risk of bowel disorders, including diverticulitis, colon and rectal cancer and irritable bowel syndrome (although bran has been found to aggravate symptoms of IBS). Few people get enough fibre. On average we eat about 12 grams of fibre a day, but we should be consuming about 18 grams. People who wish to lose weight will find that a high-fibre diet is beneficial as it provides bulk and naturally limits the amount of food eaten.

Protein

This macro-nutrient is essential for the maintenance and repair of every cell in the body, and also ensures that enzymes, hormones and antibodies function properly. Protein is made up of amino acids of which there are 20, and eight of these need to be supplied by diet. A food containing all eight amino acids is known as a "complete" or high-quality protein.

Above: Nuts contain fat as well as protein.

For vegetarians, these include eggs, dairy products as well as soya beans. Protein from plant sources, such as nuts, pasta, potatoes, legumes, cereals and rice, do not usually contain all eight amino acids and are known as "incomplete" or low-quality protein. We should aim to get 10–15 per cent of our calories from protein.

Vegetarians are often asked where they get their protein and lack of this nutrient can be a concern for those cutting out meat and fish from their diet. Yet in reality

Below: Buckwheat pasta is a "complete" protein.

most people eat too much protein and deficiency is virtually unheard of. In fact, an excess of protein can be detrimental rather than beneficial to health. High-protein foods such as dairy products and nuts are a source of fat, and have been found to leach calcium from the body, which increases the risk of osteoporosis. It is also a common misconception that vegetarians have to meticulously combine protein foods in every meal to achieve the correct balance of amino acids. Nutritionists now believe that provided a varied diet of grains, legumes, dairy produce, eggs and vegetables is eaten on a daily basis, intentionally combining proteins is unnecessary.

How to Increase Your Fibre Intake

• Base your diet on wholemeal bread and pasta, brown rice and fruit and vegetables. Refined and processed foods contain less fibre and nutrients.

• Start the day with a wholegrain cereal, such as porridge or bran flakes.

• Eat plenty of dried fruit – add it to breakfast cereals, natural yogurt or use to make a compote.

• Add beans and lentils to salads and soups to boost their fibre content.

• Avoid peeling fruits and vegetables, if possible, as the skins contain valuable fibre.

Fats

A small amount of fat in the diet is essential for health. Fat not only provides vitamins A, D and E and essential fatty acids that cannot be made in the body, but also contributes greatly to the taste, texture and palatability of food. It contains a high number of calories, and should make up no more than 30 per cent of your diet. The type of fat is as crucial as the quantity.

Saturated fat (found mainly in dairy products in the vegetarian diet) has been associated with an increased risk of cancer and coronary heart disease. Eating too much saturated fat can raise blood cholesterol levels and lead to narrowed arteries, more so than eating foods such as eggs that are high in cholesterol.

Left: Rapeseed oil, which like olive and sesame oils is a monounsaturated fat and can help to reduce the levels of cholesterol in the body, also contains Omega-3 or linolenic acid, which is thought to reduce the risk of heart disease.

Unsaturated fats, both polyunsaturated and monounsaturated, can help to reduce harmful "LDL" cholesterol (the type that furs up arteries) and, importantly, increase the beneficial "HDL" cholesterol, which is thought to reduce cholesterol levels in the body. Mono-unsaturated fats, such as olive oil, sesame oil and rapeseed oil are less vulnerable to oxidation than polyunsaturated fats. Polyunsaturated fats provide essential fatty acids, omega-3

and 6. Omega-3 (linolenic acid), which is found in walnuts, soya beans, wheatgerm and rapeseed oil, has been found to reduce the risk of heart disease, while omega-6 (linoleic acid), in nuts, seeds and oils are thought to reduce blood cholesterol.

Below: Parmesan cheese has a strong flavour, so it can be used in moderation.

How to Reduce Dietary Fat

While a vegetarian diet is often lower in fat than one based on meat, it is very easy to eat too many dairy products, oil-laden salad dressings and sauces and high-fat ready-meals. Here are a few simple ways to reduce fat in your diet:

• Use strong, mature cheese, such as Parmesan – only a small amount is need to add flavour to a dish

• Try making low-fat salad dressings using miso, orange juice, yogurt, herbs, spices or tomato juice in place of oils

• Stir-fry foods using only a little oil. For best results make sure the wok/frying pan is very hot before adding the oil

• Avoid blended oils as they can contain coconut or palm oil which are both saturated fats

• Opt for low-fat cheeses, such as cottage, curd or mozzarella instead of high-fat cheeses, such as Cheddar

• Use low-fat yogurt instead of cream in cooked recipes. Stir in a spoonful of cornflour (mixed to a paste with a little water) to prevent the yogurt curdling when heated

• Choose complex carbohydrates, including potatoes, pasta, brown rice and beans, in preference to high-fat protein foods

Above: Use naturally low-fat cheeses, such as cottage cheese, curd cheese, ricotta and quark.

Plums

QUINCE

Fragrant, with a thin, yellow or green skin. These knobbly fruits, which can be either apple- or pear-shaped, are always cooked. Their high pectin content means that they are good for jellies and, in Spain and France, quinces are used to make a fruit paste that is served with soft cheeses.

Buying and Storing: Look for smooth ripe fruits that are not too soft. Quinces keep well and can be stored in a bowl in your kitchen or living room. They will fill the room with their delicious scent.

Health Benefits: Quinces are rich in soluble fibre and pectin. They also calm the stomach and allay sickness.

Plums should be just firm, and not too soft, with shiny, smooth skin that has a slight "bloom". Store ripe plums in the fridge. Unripe fruits can be kept at room temperature for a few days to ripen. Plums relieve constipation and are thought to stimulate the nerves.

Yellow, pear-shaped quince

Dried Fruit

A useful source of energy, dried fruit is higher in calories than fresh fruit, and packed with vitamins and minerals. The drying process boosts the levels of vitamin C, beta carotene, potassium and iron. Apricots and prunes are the most popular types, but dried apple rings, cherries and peaches are also available. Sulphur, often used as a preservative in dried fruits, is best avoided, especially by people who suffer from asthma. Look for unsulphured fruit.

Stoning Fruit

1 To remove the stone from peaches, apricots or plums, cut around the middle of the fruit down to the stone with a paring knife. Twist each half of the fruit in opposite directions.

2 Prize out the stone using the tip of the knife and discard. Rub the cut flesh with lemon juice.

Citrus Fruits

Juicy and brightly coloured, citrus fruits such as oranges, grapefruit, lemons and limes are best known for their sweet, slightly sour juice, which is rich in vitamin C. They are invaluable in the kitchen, adding an aromatic acidity to many dishes, from soups and sauces to puddings and pies. Buy organic fruit when you can, and eat within a week or two.

ORANGES

Best eaten as soon as they are peeled, oranges start to lose vitamin C from the moment they are cut. Thin-skinned oranges tend to be the juiciest.

Popular varieties include the Navel (named after the belly button-type spot at the flower end), which contains no pips and so is good for slicing; sweet, juicy Jaffa and Valencia; and Seville, a sour orange used to make marmalade.

The outermost layer of the orange rind can be removed using a vegetable peeler or paring knife. This thin rind contains aromatic oils, which give a delightful perfumed flavour to both savoury and sweet dishes.

Oranges

GRAPEFRUIT

The flesh of the grapefruit ranges in colour from vivid pink and ruby red to white; the pink and red varieties are sweeter. Heavier fruits are likely to be juicier. Served juiced, halved or cut into slices, grapefruit can provide a refreshing start to the day. The fruit also adds a refreshing tang to salads or a contrast to rich foods. Cooking or grilling mellows the tartness, but keep cooking times brief to preserve the nutrients. A glass of grapefruit juice before bed is said to promote sleep.

LEMONS

Both the juice and rind of this essential cooking ingredient can be used to enliven salad dressings, vegetables, marinades, sauces and biscuits. Lemon juice can also be used to prevent some fruits and vegetables from discolouring when cut. Lemons should be deep yellow in colour, firm and heavy for their size, with no hint of green in the skin as this is a sign of immaturity, while a thin, smooth skin is a sign of juicy flesh. A slice of lemon in hot water cleanses the system and invigorates the whole body.

Citrus Nutrients

Eating an orange a day will generally supply an adult's requirement for vitamin C, but citrus fruits also contain phosphorus, potassium, calcium, beta carotene and fibre. Pectin, a soluble fibre that is found in the flesh and particularly in the membranes of citrus fruit, has been shown to reduce cholesterol levels. The membranes also contain bioflavonoids, which have powerful antioxidant properties. Drink fresh fruit juice when you can, as bottled, canned and concentrated citrus juices have reduced levels of vitamin C.

Grapefruit

Lemons

With a spoonful of honey added, a hot lemon drink is an old and trusted remedy for alleviating colds and flu.

LIMES

Once considered to be rather exotic, limes are now widely available. Avoid fruits with a yellowing skin as this is a sign of deterioration. The juice has a sharper flavour than that of lemons and if you substitute limes for lemons in a recipe, you will need to use less juice. Limes are used a great deal in Asian cooking and the rind can be used to flavour curries, marinades and dips. Coriander, chillies, garlic and ginger are all natural partners.

The Powers of Vitamin C

Citrus fruit is best known for its generous vitamin C content, which is found predominantly in the flesh. An antioxidant, vitamin C has been found to thwart many forms of cancer (particularly cancer of the stomach and oesophagus) by defending body cells against harmful free radicals. Free radicals attack DNA – the cell's genetic material – causing them to mutate and possibly become cancerous.

Numerous population studies have also demonstrated that a high dietary intake of vitamin C significantly reduces the risk of death from the world's greatest killers: the heart attack and stroke. It has been found both to lower harmful LDL cholesterol in the body and to raise beneficial HDL cholesterol. It does this by converting LDL cholesterol into bile acids, which are normally excreted. If vitamin C is in short supply, LDL cholesterol accumulates in the body.

The ability of vitamin C to boost the immune system by helping to fight viruses is well documented. It can be particularly beneficial for infections of the urinary tract and the herpes simplex virus. Researchers are in two minds as to whether vitamin C actually prevents colds but they certainly agree that it can lessen the severity and length of colds and flu. It also boosts the body's ability to absorb iron from food.

Vitamin C is destroyed by heat as well as being water soluble, and is therefore easily lost in cooking. If fruits are cut some time before eating, much of their vitamin C content will also be lost.

Limes are a good source of vitamin C.

Grating Citrus Rind

1 To remove long, thin shreds of rind, use a zester. Scrape it along the surface of the fruit, applying firm pressure.

2 For finer shreds, use a grater. Rub the fruit over the fine cutters to remove the rind without any of the white pith.

Cutting Fine Strips or Julienne

1 Using a vegetable peeler, remove strips of orange rind making sure the white pith is left behind on the fruit.

2 Stack several strips of citrus rind and, using a sharp knife, cut them into fine strips or julienne.

Buying and Storing: Look for plump, firm citrus fruit that feels heavy for its size, and has a smooth thin skin; this indicates that the flesh is juicy. Fruits with bruises, brown spots, green patches (or yellow patches on limes) and soft, squashy skin should be avoided, as should dry, wrinkled specimens. Citrus fruits can be kept at room temperature for a few days but if you want to keep them longer, they are best stored in the fridge and eaten within two weeks. Most citrus fruits are waxed or sprayed with fungicides so scrub them thoroughly to remove any residues. If you can, buy organic or unwaxed fruit.

COOK'S TIPS

• *Rolling citrus fruit firmly over a work surface or in the palms of your hands will help you extract the maximum amount of juice from the fruit.*

• *Limes and lemons will yield more juice if cut lengthways, rather than horizontally.*

RADISHES

There are several types of this peppery-
flavoured vegetable, which is a member of
the cruciferous family. The round ruby red
variety is most familiar; the longer, white-
tipped type has a milder taste. Mooli or
daikon radishes are white and very long;
they can weigh up to several kilos or
pounds. Radishes can be used to add
flavour and a crunchy texture to salads
and stir-fries. A renowned diuretic,
radishes also contain vitamin C.

*Jerusalem
artichokes*

Radishes

Mooli

HORSERADISH

This pungent root is never eaten as
a vegetable. It is usually grated and mixed
with cream or oil and vinegar, and served
as a culinary accompaniment. It is
effective in clearing blocked sinuses.

Buying and Storing: Seek out bright,
firm, unwrinkled root vegetables and
tubers, which do not have soft
patches. When possible, choose
organically grown produce, and buy
in small quantities to ensure
freshness. Store root
vegetables in a cool,
dark place.

Horseradish

Basic Vegetable Stock

Stock is easy to make at home and is a
healthier option than shop-bought stock.
It can be stored in the fridge for up to
four days. Alternatively, it can be prepared
in large quantities and frozen.

INGREDIENTS
*15ml/1 tbsp olive oil
1 potato, chopped
1 carrot, chopped
1 onion, chopped
1 celery stick, chopped
2 garlic cloves, peeled
1 sprig of thyme
1 bay leaf
a few stalks of parsley
600ml/1 pint/2 1/2 cups water
salt and freshly ground black pepper*

Heat the oil in a large saucepan.
Add the vegetables and cook, covered,
for 10 minutes or until softened, stirring
occasionally. Stir in the garlic and herbs.

2 Pour the water into the pan and
bring to the boil and simmer, partially
covered, for 40 minutes. Strain, season and
use as required.

Top Tuber

There are two types of this highly
nutritious tuber; one has cream flesh,
the other orange. The orange-fleshed
variety has a higher nutritional content
because it is richer in the antioxidant
beta carotene, but both types contain
potassium, fibre and vitamin C, as well
as providing plenty of sustained
energy. Sweet potatoes are thought to
cleanse and detoxify the body and can
boost poor circulation. When cooked,
the cream-fleshed variety has a drier
texture. Both are suited to mashing,
baking and roasting.

Brassicas and Green Leafy Vegetables

This large group of vegetables boasts an extraordinary number of health-giving properties. Brassicas range from the crinkly-leafed Savoy cabbage to the small, walnut-sized Brussels sprout. Green, leafy vegetables include spinach, spring greens and Swiss chard.

Broccoli

BROCCOLI

This nutritious vegetable should be a regular part of everyone's diet. Two types are commonly available: purple-sprouting, which has fine, leafy stems and a delicate head, and calabrese, the more substantial variety with a tightly budded top and thick stalk. Choose broccoli that has bright, compact florets. Yellowing florets, a limp woody stalk and a pungent smell are an indication of overmaturity. Trim stalks before cooking, though young stems can be eaten, too. Serve raw in salads or with a dip. If you cook broccoli, steam or stir-fry it to preserve the nutrients and keep the cooking time brief to retain the vivid green colour and crisp texture.

Health Benefits: Broccoli is a member of the cruciferous family, which studies have shown to be particularly effective in fighting cancer of the lung, colon and breast. Sulphur compounds, found in broccoli, stimulate the production of anti-cancer enzymes, which prevent the growth of tumours and inhibit the spread of existing tumours. Raw broccoli contains almost as much calcium as milk and also provides plenty of B vitamins, vitamin C, iron, folate, zinc and potassium.

CAULIFLOWER

The cream-coloured compact florets should be encased in large, bright green leaves. To get the most nutrients from a cauliflower, eat it raw, or bake or steam lightly. Cauliflower has a mild flavour and is delicious tossed in a vinaigrette dressing or combined with tomatoes and spices. Overcooked cauliflower is unpleasant and has a sulphurous taste.

Health Benefits: This creamy white cruciferous vegetable has many cancer-fighting qualities particularly against cancer of the lung and colon. Cauliflower also contains vitamin C, folate and potassium and is used in natural medicine as a blood purifier and laxative.

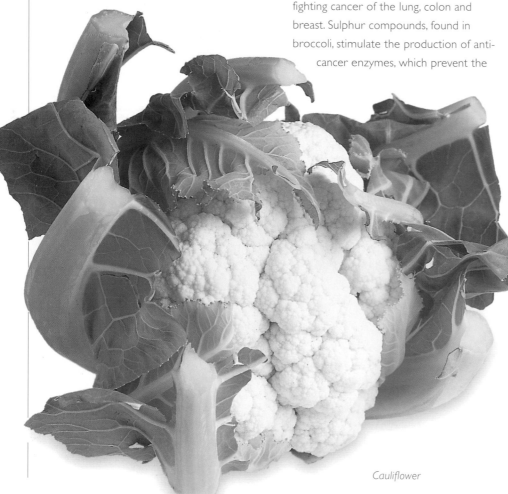

Cauliflower

Preparing Broccoli

Trim the stalks from broccoli and divide it into florets before using. The stems of young broccoli can be sliced and eaten, too.

puréed into garlic-laden dips. It is not essential to salt aubergines to remove any bitterness; however, this method prevents the absorption of excessive amounts of oil during frying.

Buying and Storing: When buying, look for small to medium-size aubergines, which have sweet, tender flesh. Large specimens with a shrivelled skin are overmature and are likely to be bitter and tough. Store in the fridge for up to two weeks.

Health Benefits: An excellent source of vitamin C, aubergines also contain moderate amounts of iron and potassium, calcium and B vitamins. They also contain bioflavonoids, which help prevent strokes and reduce the risk of certain cancers.

Bird's eye chillies

Serrano chillies

Habanero chillies

CHILLIES

Native to America, this member of the capsicum family now forms an important part of many cuisines, including Indian, Thai, Mexican, South American and African. There are more than 200 different types of chilli, ranging from the long, narrow Anaheim to the lantern-shaped and incredibly hot Habanero. Red chillies are not necessarily hotter than green ones – but they will probably have ripened for longer in the sun. The heat in chillies comes from capsaicin, a compound found in the seeds, white membranes and, to a lesser extent, in the flesh. Chillies range in potency from the mild and flavourful to the blisteringly hot. Dried chillies tend to be hotter than fresh. Smaller chillies, such as Bird's eye chillies, contain proportionately more seeds and membrane, which makes them more potent than larger ones. It is very

Red and green chillies

Jalapeño chillies

important to take care when using chillies and to wash your hands afterwards as they can irritate the skin and eyes.

Buying and Storing: Choose unwrinkled bright, firm chillies and store in the fridge.

Health Benefits: Chillies contain more vitamin C than an orange and are a good source of beta carotene, folate, potassium and vitamin E. They stimulate the release of endorphins, the body's "feel-good" chemicals and are a powerful decongestant, helping to open sinuses and air passages. Chillies stimulate the body and improve circulation, but if eaten to excess can irritate the stomach.

Chilli Boost

For an instant uplift, sprinkle some dried crushed chilli on your food. The chilli will stimulate the release of endorphins, which are the body's "feel-good" chemicals.

Handle chillies with care as they can irritate the skin and eyes. It is advisable to wear gloves when preparing chillies.

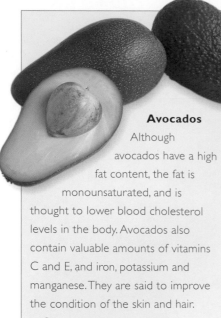

Avocados

Although avocados have a high fat content, the fat is monounsaturated, and is thought to lower blood cholesterol levels in the body. Avocados also contain valuable amounts of vitamins C and E, and iron, potassium and manganese. They are said to improve the condition of the skin and hair.

Once cut, avocados should be brushed with lemon or lime juice to prevent discoloration. They are usually eaten raw. Avocado halves can be dressed with a vinaigrette, or filled with soured cream sprinkled with cayenne pepper, or hummus. Slices or chunks of avocado are delicious in salads. In Mexico, where they grow in abundance, there are countless dishes based on avocados. Guacamole is the best known, but they are also used in soups and stews.

PEPPERS

Like chillies, sweet peppers are also members of the capsicum family. They range in colour from green through to orange, yellow, red and even purple. Green peppers are fully developed but not completely ripe, which can make them difficult to digest. They have refreshing, juicy flesh with a crisp texture. Other colours of peppers are more mature, have sweeter flesh, and are more digestible than less ripe green peppers. Roasting or chargrilling peppers will enhance their sweetness. They can also be stuffed, sliced into salads or steamed.

Buying and Storing: Choose peppers that are firm and glossy with an unblemished skin and store in the fridge for up to a week.

Health Benefits: Sweet peppers contain significant amounts of vitamin C, as well as beta carotene, some B complex vitamins, calcium, phosphorus and iron.

Peeling Peppers

1 Roast the peppers under a hot grill for 12–15 minutes, turning regularly until the skin is charred and blistered.

3 Put the peppers in a plastic bag and leave until cool – the steam will encourage the skin to peel away easily.

2 Alternatively, place on a baking tray and roast in an oven preheated to 200°C/400°F/Gas 6 for 20–30 minutes until blackened and blistered.

4 Peel off the skin, then slice in half. Remove the core and scrape out any remaining seeds. Slice or chop according to the recipe.

Peppers

Lamb's lettuce

Lamb's lettuce

This tiny lettuce has a cluster of small, rounded, velvety leaves with a delicate flavour. Serve on its own or mix with other leaves.

SALAD LEAVES

There is a great variety of different salad leaves that are now readily available.

Radicchio

A member of the chicory family, radicchio has deep-red, tightly packed leaves that have a bitter peppery flavour. It is good in salads and can be sautéed or roasted.

Rocket

Classified as a herb, rocket is a popular addition to salads, or it can be served as a starter with thin shavings of Parmesan cheese. It has a strong, peppery flavour, which is more robust when wild. Lightly steamed rocket has a milder flavour than the raw leaves but it is equally delicious.

Sorrel

Rocket

Sorrel

The long pointed leaves of sorrel have a refreshing, sharp flavour that is best when mixed with milder tasting leaves. It contains oxalic acid which, when cooked, inhibits the absorption of iron. Sorrel is an effective diuretic.

Watercress

The hot, peppery flavour of watercress complements milder tasting leaves and is

Watercress

classically combined with fresh orange. It does not keep well and is best used within two days of purchase. Watercress is a member of the cruciferous family and shares its cancer-fighting properties.

Buying and Storing: Salad leaves are best when they are very fresh and do not keep well. Avoid leaves that are wilted, discoloured or shrivelled. Store in the fridge, unwashed, for between 2 days and 1 week, depending on the variety. As salad leaves are routinely sprayed with pesticides, they should be washed thoroughly, but gently, to avoid damaging the leaves, and then dried in a kitchen cloth. Better still, choose organically grown produce.

Health Benefits: Although all types of salad leaves are about 90 per cent water, they contain useful amounts of vitamins and minerals, particularly folate, iron and the antioxidants, vitamin C and beta carotene. The outer, darker leaves tend to be more nutritious than the paler leaves in the centre. More importantly, like other green, leafy vegetables, their antioxidant content has been found to guard against the risk of many cancers. Salad leaves are usually eaten raw when the nutrients are at their strongest. Lettuce is reputed to have a calming, sedative effect.

Herbs

Herbs have been highly prized by natural practitioners for centuries because, in spite of their low nutritional value, they possess many reputed healing qualities. In cooking, herbs can make a significant difference to the flavour and aroma of a dish and they have the ability to enliven the simplest of meals. Fresh herbs can easily be grown at home in the garden, or in a pot or window box.

Chives and bay leaves

BASIL

This delicate aromatic herb is widely used in Italian and Thai cooking. The leaves bruise easily, so are best used whole or torn, rather than cut with a knife. Basil is said to have a calming effect on the stomach, easing constipation, sickness and cramps, and aiding digestion.

BAY LEAVES

These dark-green, glossy leaves are best left to dry for a few days before use. They have a robust, spicy flavour and are an essential ingredient in bouquet garni. Studies show that bay has a restorative effect on the digestive system.

CHIVES

A member of the onion family, chives have a milder flavour and are best used as a garnish, snipped over egg or potato dishes, or added to salads or flans. Like onions, chives are an antiseptic and act as a digestive.

CORIANDER

Warm and spicy, coriander is popular in Indian and Thai curries, stir-fries and salads. It looks similar to flat leaf parsley but its taste is completely different. It is often sold with its root intact. The root has a more intense flavour than the leaves and can be used in curry pastes. Coriander is

Basil

Using Dried Herbs

Although fresh herbs have the best flavour and appearance, dried herbs can be a convenient and useful alternative, especially in the winter months when some fresh herbs are not available.

• A few dried herbs such as basil, dill, mint and parsley do not dry well, losing most of their flavour.

• Oregano, thyme, marjoram and bay retain their flavour when dried and are useful substitutes for fresh.

• Dried herbs have a more concentrated flavour than fresh, so much less is required – usually a third to a half as much as fresh.

• When using dried herbs in cooking, always allow sufficient time for them to rehydrate and soften.

• Dried herbs do little for uncooked dishes, but are useful for flavouring marinades, and are good in slow-cooked stews and soups.

• When buying dried herbs, they should look bright, not faded and, because light spoils their flavour and shortens shelf-life, store in sealed, airtight jars in a cool, dark place.

Wheat flour (left) and malted brown flour, which contains flour from malted wheat grains. Stoneground versions are available

retains all the valuable nutrients. It produces slightly heavier breads, cakes and pastries than white flour, but can be combined with white flour to make lighter versions, although, of course, the nutritional value will not be as high.

SEITAN

Used as a meat replacement, seitan is made from wheat gluten and has a firm, chewy texture. It can be found in the chiller cabinet of health food shops. Seitan has a neutral flavour that benefits from marinating. Slice or cut into chunks and stir-fry, or add to stews and pasta sauces during the last few minutes of cooking time. Seitan does not need to be cooked for long, just heated through.

Buying and Storing: Buy wheat-based foods from shops with a high turnover of stock. Wheat berries can be kept for around 6 months, but wholewheat flour should be used within 3 months, as its oils turn rancid. Always decant grains into airtight containers and store in a cool, dark place. Wheat germ deteriorates very quickly at room temperature and should be stored in an airtight container in the fridge for no more than a month.

Health Benefits: Wheat is most nutritious when it is unprocessed and in its whole form. (When milled into white flour, wheat loses a staggering 80 per cent of its nutrients.) Wheat is an excellent source of dietary fibre, the B vitamins and vitamin E, as well as iron, selenium and zinc. Fibre is the most discussed virtue of whole wheat and most of this is concentrated in the bran. Eating one or more spoonfuls of bran a day is recommended to relieve constipation. Numerous studies show fibre to be effective in inhibiting colon and rectal cancer, varicose veins, haemorrhoids and obesity. Phytoestrogens found in wholegrains may also ward off breast cancer. On the negative side, wheat is also a well-known allergen and triggers coeliac disease, a gluten intolerance.

Seitan

Rice

Throughout Asia, a meal is considered incomplete without rice. It is a staple food for over half the world's population, and almost every culture has its own repertoire of rice dishes, ranging from risottos to pilaffs. What's more, this valuable food provides a good source of vitamins and minerals, as well as a steady supply of energy.

White and brown long grain rice

Jasmine fragrant rice

LONG GRAIN RICE

The most widely used type of rice is long grain rice, where the grain is five times as long as it is wide. Long grain brown rice has had its outer husk removed, leaving the bran and germ intact, which gives it a chewy nutty flavour. It takes longer to cook than white rice but contains more fibre, vitamins and minerals. Long grain white rice has had its husk, bran and germ removed, taking most of the nutrients with them and leaving a bland-flavoured rice that is light and fluffy when cooked. It is often whitened with chalk, talc or other preservatives, so rinsing is essential. Easy-cook long grain white rice, sometimes called parboiled or converted rice, has been steamed under pressure. This process hardens the grain and makes it difficult to overcook, and some nutrients are transferred from the bran and germ into the kernel during this process. Easy-cook brown rice cooks more quickly than normal brown rice.

JASMINE RICE

This rice has a soft, sticky texture and a delicious, mildly perfumed flavour – which accounts for its other name, fragrant rice. It is a long grain rice that is widely used in Thai cooking, where its delicate flavour tempers strongly spiced food.

Cooking Long Grain Brown Rice

There are many methods and opinions on how to cook rice. The absorption method is one of the simplest and retains valuable nutrients, which would otherwise be lost in cooking water that is drained away.

Different types of rice have different powers of absorption, however the general rule of thumb for long grain rice is to use double the quantity of water to rice. For example, use 1 cup of rice to 2 cups of water. 200g/7oz/1 cup long grain rice is sufficient for about four people as a side dish.

1 Rinse the rice in a sieve under cold, running water. Place in a heavy-based saucepan and add the measured cold water. Bring to the boil, uncovered, then reduce the heat and stir the rice. Add salt, to taste, if you wish.

2 Cover the pan with a tight-fitting lid. Simmer for 25–35 minutes, without removing the lid, until the water is absorbed and the rice tender. Remove from the heat and leave to stand, covered, for 5 minutes before serving.

Red rice

Wild rice

RED RICE

This rice comes from the Camargue in France and has a distinctive chewy texture and a nutty flavour. It is an unusually hard grain, which although it takes about an hour to cook, retains its shape. Cooking intensifies its red colour, making it a distinctive addition to salads and stuffings.

WILD RICE

This is not a true rice but an aquatic grass grown in North America. It has dramatic, long, slender brown-black grains that have a nutty flavour and chewy texture. It takes longer to cook than most types of rice – from 35–60 minutes, depending on whether you like it chewy or tender – but you can reduce the cooking time by soaking it in water overnight. Wild rice is extremely nutritious. It contains all eight essential amino acids and is particularly rich in lysine. It is a good source of fibre, low in calories and gluten free. Use in stuffings, serve plain or mix with other rices in pilaffs and rice salads.

BASMATI RICE

This is a slender, long grain rice, which is grown in the foothills of the Himalayas. It is aged for a year after harvest, giving it a characteristic light, fluffy texture and aromatic flavour. Its name means "fragrant".

Both white and brown types of basmati rice are available. Brown basmati contains more nutrients, and has a slightly nuttier flavour than the white variety. Widely used in Indian cooking, basmati rice has a cooling effect on hot and spicy curries. It is also excellent for biryanis and for rice salads, when you want very light, fluffy separate grains.

White and brown basmati rice

Quick Ways to Flavour Rice

• Cook brown rice in vegetable stock with sliced dried apricots. Sauté an onion in a little oil and add ground cumin, coriander and fresh chopped chilli, then mix in the cooked rice.

• Add raisins and toasted almonds to saffron-infused rice.

Lemon Barley Water

INGREDIENTS

225g/8oz/1 cup pearl barley
1.75 litres/3 pints/7½ cups water
grated rind of 1 lemon
50g/2oz/¼ cup golden caster sugar
juice of 2 lemons

1 Rinse the barley, then place in a large saucepan and cover with the water. Bring to the boil, then reduce the heat and simmer gently for 20 minutes, skimming off any scum from time to time. Remove the pan from the heat.

2 Add the lemon rind and sugar to the pan, stir well and leave to cool. Strain, and add the lemon juice.

3 Taste the lemon barley water and add more sugar, if necessary. Serve chilled with ice and slices of lemon.

QUINOA

Hailed as the supergrain of the future, quinoa (pronounced "keen-wa") is a grain of the past. It was called "the mother grain" by the Incas, who cultivated it for hundreds of years, high in the Andes, solely for their own use.

Nowadays, quinoa is widely available. The tiny, bead-shaped grains have a mild, slightly bitter taste and firm texture. It is cooked in the same way as rice, but the grains quadruple in size, becoming translucent with an unusual white outer ring. Quinoa is useful for making stuffings, pilaffs, bakes and breakfast cereals.

Health Benefits: Quinoa's supergrain status hails from its rich nutritional value. Unlike other grains, quinoa is a complete protein because it contains all eight essential amino acids. It is an excellent source of calcium, potassium and zinc as well as iron, magnesium and B vitamins. It is particularly valuable for people with coeliac disease as it is gluten-free.

MILLET

Although millet is usually associated with bird food, it is a highly nutritious grain. It once rivalled barley as the main food of Europe and remains a staple ingredient in many parts of the world, including Africa, China and India. Its mild flavour makes it an ideal accompaniment to spicy stews and curries, and it can be used as a base for pilaffs or milk puddings. The tiny, firm grains can also be flaked or ground into flour. Millet is gluten-free, so it is a useful food for people with coeliac disease. The flour can be used for baking, but needs to be combined with high-gluten flours to make leavened bread.

Health Benefits: Millet is an easily digestible grain. It contains more iron than other grains and is a good source of zinc, calcium, manganese and B vitamins. It is believed to be beneficial to those suffering from candidiasis, a fungal infection caused by the yeast *Candida albicans*.

Millet

Amaranth

LESSER-KNOWN GRAINS

There are several other grains that deserve a mention, as they are not only becoming more popular, but also are often far richer in nutrients than their better-known counterparts.

Amaranth

This plant, which is native to Mexico, is unusual in that it can be eaten as both a vegetable and a grain. Like quinoa, amaranth is considered a supergrain due to its excellent nutritional content. The tiny pale seed or "grain" has a strong and distinctive, peppery flavour. It is best used in stews and soups, or it can be ground into flour to make bread, pastries and biscuits. The flour is gluten-free and has to be mixed with wheat or another flour that contains gluten to make leavened bread. Amaranth leaves are similar to spinach and can be cooked or eaten raw in salads.

Health Benefits: Although its taste may take some getting used to, the nutritional qualities of amaranth more than make up for it. It has more protein than pulses and is rich in amino acids, particularly lysine. Amaranth is also high in iron and calcium.

Kamut

An ancient relative of wheat, this grain has long, slender, brown kernels with a creamy, nutty flavour. It is as versatile as wheat and, when ground into flour, can be used to make pasta, breads, cakes and pastry. Puffed kamut cereals and kamut crackers are available in health food shops.

BUCKWHEAT

In spite of its name, buckwheat is not a type of wheat, but is actually related to the rhubarb family. Available plain or toasted, it has a nutty, earthy flavour. It is a staple food in Eastern Europe as well as Russia, where the triangular grain is milled into a speckled-grey flour and used to make blini. The flour is also used in Japan for soba noodles and in Italy for pasta. Buckwheat pancakes are popular in parts of the USA and France. The whole grain, which is also known as kasha, makes a fine porridge or a creamy pudding.

Health Benefits: Like quinoa, buckwheat is a complete protein. It contains all eight essential amino acids as well as rutin, which aids circulation and helps treat high blood pressure. It is an excellent, sustaining cereal, rich in both iron and some of the B complex vitamins. It is also reputed to be good for the lungs, the kidneys and the bladder. Buckwheat is gluten-free, and so is useful for people who suffer from coeliac disease.

Above, plain buckwheat, buckwheat flour and toasted buckwheat

Health Benefits: Kamut has a higher nutritional value than wheat and is easier to digest. Although it contains gluten, people suffering from coeliac disease have found that they can tolerate the grain if eaten in moderation.

Sorghum

This grain is best known for its thick sweet syrup, which is used in cakes and desserts. The grain is similar to millet and is an important, extremely nutritious staple food in Africa and India. It can be used much like rice, and when ground into flour is used to make unleavened bread.

Health Benefits: Sorghum is a useful source of calcium, iron and B vitamins.

Spelt

This is one of the most ancient cultivated wheats and, because of its high nutritional value, is becoming more widely available. Spelt grain looks very similar to wheat and the flour can be substituted for wheat flour in bread.

Health Benefits: Spelt is richer in vitamins and minerals than wheat, and they are in a more readily digestible form. Although spelt contains gluten, it usually can be tolerated in moderate amounts by people suffering from coeliac disease.

Triticale

A hybrid of wheat and rye, triticale was created by Swedish researchers in 1875. It has a sweet, nutty taste and chewy texture and can be used in the

Kamut

Spelt grain and flour

same way as rice, and is ground into flour. It contains more protein than wheat but has less gluten and may need to be mixed with other flours when baking. Triticale flakes can be used in breakfast cereals and crumbles.

Health Benefits: Triticale contains significant amounts of calcium, iron and B vitamins. It is particularly rich in lysine.

Buying and Storing: To ensure freshness, buy grains in small quantities from a shop with a high turnover of stock. Grains can be affected by heat and moisture, and easily become rancid. Store in a dry, cool, dark place.

How to Cook Grains

Grains can be simply boiled in water but, to enhance their flavour, first cook them in a little oil for a few minutes. When they are well coated in oil, add two or three times their volume of water or stock. Bring to the boil, then simmer, covered, until the water is absorbed and the grains are tender. Do not disturb the grains while they are cooking. Other flavourings, such as chopped herbs and whole or ground spices, can be added to the cooking liquid.

Fabulous Fibre

Whole grains are one of the few food groups to contain both soluble and insoluble fibre. The former is prevalent in oats and rye, while wheat, rice and corn contain insoluble fibre. Both are fundamental to good health and may prevent constipation, ulcers, colitis, colon and rectal cancer, heart disease, diverticulitis and irritable bowel syndrome. Soluble fibre slows down the absorption of energy from the gut, which means there are no sudden demands on insulin, making it especially important for diabetics.

Tempeh

TVP

Textured vegetable protein, or TVP, is a useful meat replacement and is usually bought in dry chunks or as mince. Made from processed soya beans, TVP is very versatile and readily absorbs the strong flavours of ingredients such as herbs, spices and vegetable stock. It is inexpensive and is a convenient store-cupboard item. TVP needs to be rehydrated in boiling water or vegetable stock, and can be used in stews and curries, or as a filling for pies.

be soaked until pliable before use. Beancurd skins should be soaked for an hour or two and can be used to wrap a variety of fillings.

Beancurd sticks need to be soaked for several hours or overnight. They can be chopped and added to soups, stir-fries and casseroles.

Tofu Fruit Fool

I Place a packet of silken tofu in the bowl of a food processor. Add some soft fruit or berries – for example, strawberries, raspberries or blackberries.

2 Process the mixture to form a smooth purée, then sweeten to taste with a little honey, maple syrup or maize malt syrup.

Marinated Tofu Kebabs

Tofu is relatively tasteless but readily takes on other flavours. It is at its best when marinated in aromatic oils, soy sauce, spices and herbs.

I Cut a block of tofu into 1cm/½in cubes and marinate in a mixture of groundnut oil, sesame oil, soy sauce, crushed garlic, grated fresh root ginger and honey for at least 1 hour.

2 Thread the cubes of tofu on to skewers with chunks of courgettes, onions and mushrooms. Brush with the marinade and grill or barbecue until golden, turning occasionally.

Soya flour

SOYA FLOUR

This is a finely ground, high-protein flour, which is also gluten-free. It is often mixed with other flours in bread and pastries, adding a pleasant nuttiness, or it can be used as a thickener in sauces.

Buying and Storing: Store TVP and soya flour in an airtight container in a cool, dry, dark place.

SOY SAUCE

This soya by-product originated over 2,000 years ago and the recipe has changed little since then. It is made by combining crushed soya beans with wheat, salt, water and a yeast-based culture called *koji*, and the mixture is left to ferment for between 6 months and 3 years.

There are two basic types of soy sauce: light and dark. Light soy sauce is slightly thinner in consistency and saltier. It is used in dressings and soups. Dark soy sauce is heavier and sweeter, with a more rounded flavour, and is used in marinades, stir-fries and sauces. Try to buy naturally brewed soy sauce as many other kinds are now chemically prepared to hasten the fermentation process, and may contain flavourings and colourings.

SHOYU

Made in Japan, shoyu is aged for 1–2 years to produce a full-flavoured sauce that can be used in the same way as dark soy sauce. You can buy it in health food stores and Oriental shops.

TAMARI

This form of soy sauce is a natural by-product of making miso, although it is often produced in the same way as soy sauce. Most tamari is made without wheat, which means that it is gluten-free. It has a rich, dark, robust flavour and is used in cooking or as a condiment.

Buying and Storing: Keep soy sauce, shoyu and tamari in a cool, dark place.

MISO

This thick paste is made from a mixture of cooked soya beans, rice, wheat or barley, salt and water, miso is left to ferment for up to 3 years. It can be used to add a savoury flavour to soups, stocks, stir-fries and noodle dishes, and is a staple food in Asia. There are three main types: kome, or white miso, is the lightest and sweetest; medium-strength mugi miso, which has a mellow flavour and is preferred for everyday use; and hacho miso, which is a dark chocolate colour, and has a thick texture and a strong flavour.

Soya Bean Sauces

Black bean sauce Made from fermented black soya beans, this has a rich, thick consistency and a salty, full flavour. It should always be heated before use to bring out the flavour. Fermented black beans, which Chinese cooks use to make home-made black bean sauce, can be bought in vacuum-packs or cans from Oriental shops.

Yellow bean sauce Produced from fermented yellow soya beans, this sauce has an intense flavour.

Hoisin sauce A thick red-brown sauce made from soya beans, flour, garlic, chilli, sesame oil and vinegar. Mainly intended as a marinade, it can be used as a dipping sauce.

Kecap manis An Indonesian-style dark, sweet soy sauce, which can be found in Oriental shops.

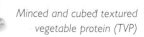

Minced and cubed textured vegetable protein (TVP)

Buying and Storing: Miso keeps well and can be stored for several months, but should be kept in the fridge once it has been opened.

Health Benefits: Soya is one of today's healthiest foods. Rich in minerals, particularly iron and calcium, it is also low in saturated fat and is cholesterol-free. It has the ability to help reduce osteoporosis, blood pressure and blood cholesterol, and there is evidence to suggest that it can help reduce the risk of cancer.

Japanese women (whose diets are rich in soya) have a lower incidence of breast cancer than women who consume a typical Western diet. Likewise, Japanese men have a lower incidence of prostate cancer than Western men. This is thought to be because soya contains hormone-like substances called phytoestrogens.

Studies have also shown that eating miso on a regular basis can increase the body's natural resistance to radiation. Additionally, miso is said to prevent cancer of the liver, and it can also help to expel toxins from the body.

Light soy sauce (below) and dark soy sauce

Watch Point
Although soya beans and products are nutritionally beneficial, they are also common allergens and can provoke reactions such as headaches and digestive problems. Avoid eating excessive amounts of soya, and always cook sprouted soya beans before use.

Mugi miso (left) and hacho miso

Tamari (left) and shoyu

Buying and Storing: Freshness is paramount when buying eggs. Buy from a shop that has a high turnover of stock. You should reject any eggs that have a broken, dirty or damaged shell. Most eggs are date stamped, but you can easily check if an egg is fresh, by placing it in a bowl of cold water: if the egg sinks and lays flat it is fresh. The older the egg, the more it will stand on its end. A really old egg will actually float and shouldn't be eaten. Store eggs in their box in the main part of the fridge and not in a rack in the door as this can expose them to odours and damage. The shells are extremely porous, so eggs can be tainted by strong smells. Eggs should be stored large-end up for no longer than 3 weeks.

Health Benefits: Eggs have received much adverse publicity due to their high cholesterol levels. However, attention has moved away from dietary cholesterol to cholesterol that is produced in the body from saturated fats. Saturated fats are now claimed to play a bigger role in raising cholesterol levels, and as eggs are low in saturated fat, they have been somewhat reprieved. They should, however, be eaten in moderation, and people with raised cholesterol levels should take particular care. Nutritionists recommend that we eat no more than four eggs a week. Eggs provide B vitamins, especially B_{12}, vitamins A and D, iron, choline and phosphorus, and cooking does not significantly alter their nutritional content.

Quick Ideas for Eggs

• Brush beaten egg on to pastries and bread before baking to give them a golden glaze.
• For a protein boost, top Thai- or Chinese-flavoured rice or noodle dishes with strips of thin omelette.
• Turn a mixed leaf salad into a light supper dish by adding a soft-boiled egg and some half-fat mayonnaise.
• For a simple dessert, make a soufflé omelette. Separate 2 eggs and whisk the whites and yolks separately. Fold together gently and add a little sugar. Cook in the same way as a savoury omelette and serve plain or fill with fruit conserve or lemon curd.

Herb Omelette

A simple, herb-flavoured omelette is quick to cook and, served with a salad and a chunk of crusty bread, makes a nutritious, light meal. Even if you are going to serve more than one, it is better to cook individual omelettes and eat them as soon as they are ready.

INGREDIENTS

2 eggs
15ml/1 tbsp chopped fresh herbs, such as tarragon, parsley or chives
5ml/1 tsp butter
salt and freshly ground black pepper

SERVES 1

1 Lightly beat the eggs in a bowl, add the fresh herbs and season to taste.

2 Melt the butter in a heavy-based, non-stick frying pan and swirl it around to coat the base evenly.

3 Pour in the egg mixture and, as the egg sets, push the edges towards the centre using a spoon, allowing the raw egg to run on to the hot pan.

4 Cook for about 2 minutes, without stirring, until the egg is just lightly set. Quickly fold over the omelette and serve immediately.

The Store Cupboard

The following section features a diverse range of foods that can enrich and add variety to a vegetarian diet. Some ingredients may be familiar, others less so, but all are useful to keep in the store cupboard. Each of the mentioned foods comes with notes on choosing, storage and preparation, when necessary, as well as nutritional or medicinal properties.

Nuts

With the exception of peanuts, nuts are the fruits of trees. The quality and availability of fresh nuts varies with the seasons, although most types are sold dried, either whole or prepared ready for use. Shelled nuts come in many forms: they may be whole, blanched, halved, sliced, shredded, chopped, ground or toasted.

Chestnuts

ALMONDS

There are two types of almond: sweet and bitter. The best sweet varieties are the flat and slender Jordan almonds from Spain. Heart-shaped Valencia almonds from Portugal and Spain, and the flatter Californian almonds are also widely available. For the best flavour, buy shelled almonds in their skins and blanch them yourself: cover with boiling water, leave for a few minutes, then drain and the skins will peel off easily. Almonds are available ready-blanched, flaked and ground. The latter adds a richness to cakes, tarts, pastry and sauces. Bitter almonds are much smaller and are used in almond oil and essence. They should not be eaten raw as they contain traces of the lethal prussic acid.

BRAZIL NUTS

These are, in fact, seeds, and are grown mainly in the Amazon regions of Brazil and other neighbouring countries. Between 12 and 20 Brazil nuts grow, packed snugly together, in a large brown husk, hence their three-cornered wedge shape. Brazil

nuts have a sweet, milky taste and are used mainly as dessert nuts. They have a high fat content, so go rancid very quickly.

CASHEW NUTS

These are the seeds of the "cashew apple" – an evergreen tree with bright-orange fruit. Cashew nuts have a sweet flavour and crumbly texture. They make delicious nut butters, or can be sprinkled into stir-fries or over salads. They are never sold in the shell and undergo an extensive heating process that removes the seed from its outer casing.

CHESTNUTS

Raw chestnuts are not recommended as they are not only unpleasant to eat but also contain tannic acid, which inhibits the absorption of iron. Most chestnuts are imported from France and Spain and they are excellent after roasting, which complements their soft, floury texture. Unlike other nuts, they contain very little fat. Out of season, chestnuts can be bought dried, canned or puréed. Add

Blanched, whole and shelled almonds; shelled cashew nuts (in bowl); and shelled and whole Brazil nuts

Above, clockwise from left: cinnamon sticks, coriander seeds, cloves and ground cinnamon

CELERY SEEDS

These tiny brown seeds have a similar flavour to celery, but are more highly aromatic. It is important to grind or crush them before use to avoid any bitterness. Celery seeds can be used in almost any dish that calls for celery, and they add a pungent flavour to vegetarian bakes, stews, soups, sauces and egg dishes. Celery salt is a mixture of ground celery seeds, salt and other herbs. Celery seeds are carminative, relieving both flatulence and indigestion.

CHILLIES

Fresh chillies are covered in the vegetable section, but this versatile spice is also sold in dried, powdered and flaked form. Dried chillies tend to be hotter than fresh, and this is certainly true of chilli flakes, which contain both the seeds and the flesh. The best pure chilli powders do not contain added ingredients, such as onion and garlic. A powerful stimulant and expectorant, chilli also has a reputation as an aphrodisiac.

CINNAMON

This warm, comforting spice is available in sticks (quills) and ground. As the bark is difficult to grind, it is useful to keep both forms in the store cupboard. Cinnamon can enhance both sweet and savoury dishes. Use the sticks to flavour pilaffs, curries, couscous and dried fruit compotes, but remove before serving.

Ground cinnamon adds a pleasing fragrance to cakes, biscuits and fruit. Cinnamon is an effective detoxifier and cleanser, containing substances that kill bacteria and other micro-organisms.

CLOVES

The unopened bud of an evergreen tree from South-east Asia, this spice is often used in combination with cinnamon to flavour puddings, cakes and biscuits. Cloves are often used to flavour the syrup when poaching oranges, but they are also delicious with cooked apples.

Clove oil has long been used as a cure for toothache, and both its antiseptic and anaesthetic qualities can relieve pain and discomfort throughout the body.

CORIANDER

Alongside cumin, ground coriander is a key ingredient in Indian curry powders and garam masala, and in northern Europe the ivory-coloured seeds are used as a pickling spice. Coriander seeds have a sweet, earthy, burnt-orange flavour that is more pronounced than the fresh leaves. The ready-ground powder rapidly loses its flavour and aroma, so it is best to buy whole seeds, which are easily ground in a mortar using a pestle, or in a coffee grinder. Before grinding, lightly dry-roast the seeds in a frying pan to enhance their flavour. Coriander has been prescribed as a digestive for thousands of years, relieving indigestion, diarrhoea and nausea. It also has antibacterial properties.

Cumin seeds, ground cumin and (front) fenugreek

CUMIN

Extensively used in Indian curries, cumin is also a familiar component of Mexican, North African and Middle Eastern cooking. The seeds have a robust aroma and slightly bitter taste, which is tempered by dry-roasting. Black cumin seeds, which are also known as nigella, are milder and sweeter. Ground cumin can be harsh, so it is best to buy the whole seeds and grind them just before use to ensure a fresh flavour. Cumin is good in tomato- or grain-based dishes, and its digestive properties mean that it is also ideal with beans.

Fresh root ginger

GINGER

This spice is probably one of the oldest and most popular herbal medicines. The fresh root, which is spicy, peppery and fragrant, is good in both sweet and savoury dishes, adding a hot, yet refreshing, flavour to marinades, stir-fries, soups, curries, grains and fresh vegetables. It also adds warmth to poached fruit, pastries and cakes.

Ground ginger is the usual choice for flavouring cakes, biscuits and other baked goods, but finely grated fresh ginger can also be used and is equally good.

Ground ginger

FENUGREEK

This spice is commonly used in commercial curry powders, along with cumin and coriander. On its own though, fenugreek should be used in moderation because its bitter-sweet flavour, which is mellowed by dry-frying, can be quite overpowering. The seeds have a hard shell and are difficult to grind, but they can be sprouted and make a good addition to mixed leaf and bean salads, as well as sandwich fillings. Fenugreek has long been prescribed to treat stomach and intestinal disorders, and its ability to cleanse the body may help in the release of toxins.

Ginger tea, made by steeping a few slices of fresh root ginger in hot water for a few minutes, can calm and soothe the stomach after a bout of food poisoning as well as ward off colds and flu.

Pink pickled ginger

This pretty, finely sliced ginger pickle is served as an accompaniment to Japanese food and is used to flavour sushi rice.

Stem ginger

Preserved in a thick sugar syrup and sold in jars, this sweet ginger can be chopped and used in desserts, or added to cake mixtures, steamed puddings, scones, shortbread and muffins.

Buying and Storing: Fresh root ginger should look firm, thin-skinned and unblemished. Avoid withered, woody looking roots as these are likely to be dry and fibrous. Store in the fridge. Ground ginger should smell aromatic; keep in a cool, dark place.

Preparing Fresh Ginger

1 Fresh root ginger is most easily peeled using a vegetable peeler or a small, sharp paring knife.

3 Grate ginger finely – special graters can be found in Asian shops, but a box grater will do the job equally well.

2 Chop ginger using a sharp knife to the size specified in the recipe.

4 Freshly grated ginger can be squeezed to release the juice.

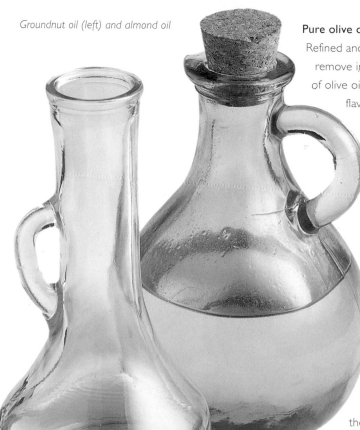

Groundnut oil (left) and almond oil

Pure olive oil
Refined and blended to remove impurities, this type of olive oil has a much lighter flavour than virgin or extra virgin olive oil and is suitable for all types of cooking. It can be used for shallow frying.

OTHER OILS
There is a wide range of light, processed oils on the market, which are all relatively taste-free and have a variety of uses in the kitchen.

Corn oil
One of the most economical and widely used vegetable oils, corn oil has a deep golden colour and a fairly strong flavour. It is suitable for cooking and frying, but should not be used for salad dressings. Corn is rich in omega-6 (linoleic) fatty acids, which are believed to reduce harmful cholesterol in the body.

Safflower oil
This is a light, all-purpose oil, which comes from the seeds of the safflower. It can be used in place of sunflower and groundnut oils, but is a little thicker and has a slightly stronger flavour. It is suitable for deep frying, but is best used with other more strongly flavoured ingredients, and is ideal for cooking spicy foods. Safflower oil contains more polyunsaturated fat than any other type of oil and it is low in saturated fat.

Sunflower oil
Perhaps the best all-purpose oil, sunflower oil is very light and almost tasteless. It is very versatile, and can be used for frying and in cooking, or to make salad dressings, when it can be combined with a stronger flavoured oil such as olive oil or walnut oil. Sunflower oil is extracted from the seeds of the sunflower. It is very high in poly-unsaturated fat and low in saturated fat.

Soya oil
This neutral flavoured, all-purpose oil, which is extracted from soya beans, is probably the most widely used oil in the world. It is useful for frying because it has a high smoking point, and remains stable at high temperatures. It is also widely used in margarines. It is rich in polyunsaturated and monounsaturated fats and low in saturates. Find a brand that is not made from genetically modified soya beans.

Groundnut oil
Also known as peanut oil, this relatively tasteless oil is useful for frying, cooking and dressing salads. Chinese peanut oil is darker in colour than groundnut oil and

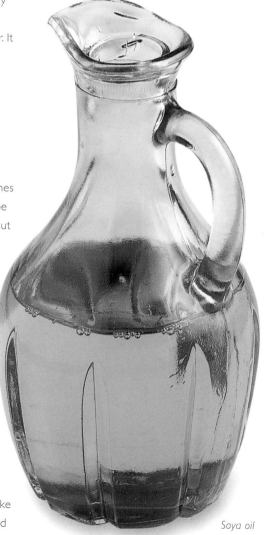

Soya oil

Quick Ideas for Marinades
• Mix olive oil with chopped fresh herbs such as parsley, chives, oregano, chervil and basil. Add a splash or two of lemon juice and season with salt and pepper.
• Combine groundnut oil, toasted sesame oil, dark soy sauce, sweet sherry, rice vinegar and crushed garlic. Use as a marinade for tofu or tempeh.

• Mix together olive oil, lemon juice, sherry, honey and crushed garlic and and use as a marinade for vegetable and halloumi kebabs.

has a more distinctive nutty flavour. It is good in Oriental salads and stir-fries. Groundnut oil has a higher percentage of monounsaturated fat than soya oil but also contains polyunsaturated fat.

Rapeseed oil

This bland-tasting, all-purpose oil, also known as canola, can be used for frying, cooking and in salad dressings. It contains a higher percentage of monounsaturated fat than any other oil, with the exception of olive oil.

Grapeseed oil

A delicate, mild flavoured oil, which does not impose on other ingredients, grapeseed oil is pressed from grape seeds left over from wine-making. It is good in cooking and for frying, and can be used to make salad dressings, especially when combined with a stronger flavoured nut or olive oil. Grapeseed oil is high in poly-unsaturated fat.

Rapeseed oil

SPECIALITY OILS

As well as the light, all-purpose oils that are used for everyday cooking, there are several richly flavoured oils that are used in small quantities, often as a flavouring ingredient in salad dressings and marinades, rather than for cooking.

Sesame oil

There are two types of sesame oil – the pale and light version that is pressed from untoasted seeds, and the rich, dark, toasted oil that is used in Oriental cuisines. The lighter oil, popular in India and the Middle East, has a mild flavour and a high smoking point and is useful for cooking. Dark sesame oil, which has a wonderfully nutty aroma and taste, is useful for flavouring marinades and stir-fries. It has a much stronger taste than either walnut oil or olive oil and is too overpowering to use in large quantities. However, it can be mixed with milder oils, such as groundnut or soya. Heating helps to intensify the aroma of toasted sesame oil, but it should never be heated for too long. Both types of sesame oil are high in polyunsaturated fat.

Walnut oil

This is an intensely flavoured oil that is delicious in salad dressings and marinades, but shouldn't be used for frying as heat diminishes its rich taste (it is also far too expensive to use in any great quantity). Instead, drizzle a little of the oil over roasted or steamed vegetables, use it to make a simple sauce for pasta, or stir into freshly cooked noodles just before serving. It can be used in small quantities, in place of some of the fat or oil in a recipe, to add flavour to cakes and biscuits, especially those that contain walnuts. Walnut oil does not keep for long and, after opening, should be kept in a cool, dark place to

Quick Ideas for Dressings and Salads

A good dressing should enhance rather than overpower the salad.

• To make a simple vinaigrette dressing, whisk together 60ml/4 tbsp extra virgin olive oil with 15ml/1 tbsp red or white wine vinegar or balsamic vinegar in a small jug. Add a pinch of sugar and 5ml/1 tsp Dijon mustard. Season to taste.

• To make a walnut oil dressing, whisk together 60ml/4 tbsp walnut oil with 15ml/1 tbsp sherry vinegar, then season to taste. This dressing is good with strong flavoured leaves, such as rocket, watercress or radicchio.

• Combine walnut oil and low-fat fromage frais or yogurt with chopped fresh flat leaf parsley. Season, then spoon the dressing over new potatoes and garnish with snipped chives and toasted chopped walnuts.

• Mix together grated fresh ginger, fresh coriander, lime juice and toasted sesame oil and pour over grated carrot. Sprinkle toasted sesame seeds over the carrot mixture.

• Mix together extra virgin olive oil and lemon juice, and spoon over warm flageolet and cannellini beans. Add chopped tomatoes and chopped fresh flat leaf parsley.

• Toss steamed broccoli florets or sugar snap peas in a dressing made from hazelnut oil, olive oil, white wine vinegar and Dijon mustard.

Breakfasts
and
Brunches

There's no better way to start the day than with a well-balanced breakfast. Base it on high carbohydrate whole foods such as cereals, grains or beans, and you not only replenish nutrients and energy stocks depleted overnight, but also set yourself up sensibly for whatever lies ahead. High-carbohydrate foods provide sustained, slow-release energy and are much more effective at fighting hunger than fry-ups or sugary cereals. Choices like Porridge with Date Purée and Pistachio Nuts, Griddled Tomatoes on Soda Bread or a fish-free Kedgeree are not only undeniably delicious, they also stave off snack attacks. Recent research suggests that those who eat a carbohydrate-based breakfast are likely to eat less during the day, perform better at school or work and find it easier to control their weight. Can't face solid food that early in the morning? Wake to a shake instead. Cleansing juices and fruit smoothies take only seconds to make, but give you energy for hours.

Banana and Strawberry Smoothie

FULL OF ENERGY-GIVING OATS and fruits, this tasty drink makes a brilliant breakfast.

INGREDIENTS

2 bananas, quartered
250g/9oz/2 cups strawberries
30ml/2 tbsp oatmeal
500g/1¼lb/2½ cups natural
    live yogurt
Serves 2

COOK'S TIP

Prepare fruit drinks just before serving to gain maximum benefit from the nutrients.

| Place the bananas, strawberries, oatmeal and yogurt in a food processor or blender and process for a few minutes until combined and creamy. Pour into tall glasses and serve.

Citrus Shake

PACKED WITH VITAMIN C, this refreshing juice is a great way to start the day.

INGREDIENTS

1 pineapple
6 oranges, peeled and chopped
juice of 1 lemon
1 pink grapefruit, peeled and
    quartered
Serves 4

1 To prepare the pineapple, cut the bottom and the spiky top off the fruit. Stand the pineapple upright and cut off the skin, removing all the spikes and as little of the flesh as possible. Lay the pineapple on its side and cut into bite-size chunks.

2 Place the pineapple, oranges, lemon juice and grapefruit in a food processor or blender and process for a few minutes until combined.

3 Press the fruit juice through a sieve to remove any pith or membranes. Serve chilled.

Cranberry and Apple Juice

THIS GINGER-FLAVOURED, CLEANSING JUICE offers a fine balance of sweet and sour flavours.

INGREDIENTS

4 eating apples
600ml/1 pint/2½ cups
    cranberry juice
2.5cm/1in piece fresh root
    ginger, peeled and sliced
Serves 4

HEALTH BENEFITS

Brightly coloured fruits, such as cranberries, contain valuable amounts of antioxidant vitamins, which are believed to have cancer-fighting properties.

1 Peel the apples, if you wish, then core and chop.

2 Pour the cranberry juice into a food processor or blender. Add the chopped apples and sliced ginger and process for a few minutes until combined and fairly smooth. Serve chilled.

Zingy Vegetable Juice

GINGER PACKS A POWERFUL punch and certainly gets you going in the morning, even if you're feeling groggy.

INGREDIENTS

1 cooked beetroot in natural
    juice, sliced
1 large carrot, sliced
4cm/1½in piece fresh root
    ginger, peeled and finely grated
2 apples, peeled, if liked,
    chopped and cored
150g/5oz/1¼ cups seedless
    white grapes
300ml/½ pint/1¼ cups fresh
    orange juice
Serves 2

1 Place the beetroot, carrot, ginger, apples, grapes and orange juice in a food processor or blender and process for a few minutes until combined and fairly smooth. Serve immediately or chill until ready to serve.

Right: Clockwise from top right, Cranberry and Apple Juice, Citrus Shake, Banana and Strawberry Smoothie, Zingy Vegetable Juice.

Griddled Pineapple and Mango on Toasted Panettone with Vanilla Yogurt

GRIDDLING CONCENTRATES the sweetness of both the pineapple and mango, giving them a caramel flavour that is complemented by the vanilla yogurt.

INGREDIENTS

1 large pineapple
1 large mango
25g/1oz/2 tbsp unsalted butter, melted
4 thick slices panettone

For the vanilla yogurt
250g/9oz/generous 1 cup Greek yogurt
30ml/2 tbsp clear honey
2.5ml/1/2 tsp ground cinnamon
a few drops natural vanilla essence, to taste

Serves 4

1 To prepare the pineapple, cut the bottom and the spiky top off the fruit. Stand the pineapple upright and cut off the skin, removing all the spikes, but as little of the flesh as possible. Lay the pineapple on its side and cut into quarters; remove the core if it is hard. Cut the pineapple into thick wedges.

HEALTH BENEFITS

Pineapple contains the powerful enzyme bromelain, which improves the digestion. It contains compounds that have an anti-inflammatory effect, so is good for people who suffer from arthritis. Pineapple has also been shown to reduce the incidence of blood clots and to ease bronchitis.

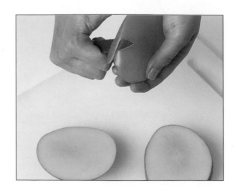

2 To prepare the mango, cut away the two thick sides of the mango as close to the stone as possible. Peel the mango, then cut the remaining flesh from the stone. Slice the fruit and discard the stone.

3 Heat a griddle pan over a medium heat. Add the pineapple and mango (you may need to do this in batches). Brush with melted butter, and cook for 8 minutes, turning once, until soft and slightly golden. Alternatively, heat the grill to high and line the rack with foil. Place the pineapple and mango on the foil, brush with butter and grill for 4 minutes on each side.

4 Meanwhile, place the yogurt in a bowl with the honey, cinnamon and vanilla and stir well.

5 Lightly toast the panettone, then serve, topped with the pineapple and mango and accompanied by the vanilla yogurt.

Oaty Pancakes with Caramel Bananas and Pecan Nuts

THESE PANCAKES ARE MORE like drop scones than the classic thin French crêpes. Bananas and pecan nuts, cooked in maple syrup, make a sweet and delicious topping.

INGREDIENTS

75g/3oz/²/3 cup plain flour

50g/2oz/¹/2 cup wholemeal flour

50g/2oz/¹/2 cup porridge oats

5ml/1 tsp baking powder

pinch of salt

25g/1oz/2 tbsp golden caster sugar

1 egg

15ml/1 tbsp sunflower oil, plus extra
    for frying

250ml/8fl oz/1 cup semi-skimmed milk

**For the caramel bananas and
    pecan nuts**

50g/2oz/4 tbsp butter

15ml/1 tbsp maple syrup

3 bananas, halved and quartered
    lengthways

25g/1oz/¹/4 cup pecan nuts

Serves 5

1 To make the pancakes, mix together the plain and wholemeal flours, oats, baking powder, salt and sugar in a bowl.

HEALTH BENEFITS

• *Pecan nuts are one of the richest sources of vitamin B$_6$, which can help relieve the symptoms of PMS (premenstrual syndrome), as well as giving our immune system a boost. However, they are high in fat, so eat in moderation.*

• *Bananas are a good source of energy, making them an excellent food to start the day. They also contain potassium, which is essential for the functioning of all the cells in our bodies.*

• *Porridge oats contain useful amounts of soluble fibre, which has been found to lower cholesterol levels in the body.*

2 Make a well in the centre of the flour mixture and add the egg, oil and a quarter of the milk. Mix well, then gradually add the rest of the milk to make a thick batter. Leave to rest for 20 minutes in the fridge.

3 Heat a large, heavy-based, lightly oiled frying pan. Using about 30ml/2 tbsp of batter for each pancake, cook 2–3 pancakes at a time. Cook for 3 minutes on each side or until golden. Keep warm while you cook the remaining 7–8 pancakes.

4 To make the caramel bananas and pecan nuts, wipe out the frying pan and add the butter. Heat gently until the butter melts, then add the maple syrup and stir well. Add the bananas and pecan nuts to the pan.

5 Cook for about 4 minutes, turning once, or until the bananas have just softened and the sauce has caramelized. To serve, place two pancakes on each of five warm plates and top with the caramel bananas and pecan nuts. Serve immediately.

Luxury Muesli

COMMERCIALLY MADE MUESLI really can't compete with this home-made version. This combination of seeds, grains, nuts and dried fruits works particularly well, but you can alter the balance of ingredients, or substitute others, if you like.

INGREDIENTS

50g/2oz/¹/2 cup sunflower seeds
25g/1oz/¹/4 cup pumpkin seeds
115g/4oz/1 cup porridge oats
115g/4oz/heaped 1 cup wheat flakes
115g/4oz/heaped 1 cup barley flakes
115g/4oz/1 cup raisins
115g/4oz/1 cup chopped
  hazelnuts, roasted
115g/4oz/¹/2 cup unsulphured dried
  apricots, chopped
50g/2oz/2 cups dried apple slices, halved
25g/1oz/¹/3 cup desiccated coconut
Serves 4

1 Put the sunflower and pumpkin seeds in a dry frying pan and cook over a medium heat for 3 minutes until golden, tossing the seeds regularly to prevent them burning.

VARIATION

Serve the muesli in a long glass layered with fresh raspberries and fromage frais. Soak the muesli first in a little water or fruit juice in order to soften it slightly.

2 Mix the toasted seeds with the remaining ingredients and leave to cool. Store in an airtight container.

HEALTH BENEFITS

• *Sunflower seeds are rich in vitamin E, which is thought to reduce the risk of heart disease.*
• *Apricots are high on the list of fruits that are considered likely to help prevent certain cancers, notably that of the lung.*

Granola

HONEY-COATED NUTS, SEEDS and oats, combined with sweet dried fruits, make an excellent and nutritious start to the day – without the additives often found in pre-packed cereals. Serve the granola with semi-skimmed milk or natural live yogurt and fresh fruit.

INGREDIENTS

115g/4oz/1 cup porridge oats
115g/4oz/1 cup jumbo oats
50g/2oz/¹/2 cup sunflower seeds
25g/1oz/2 tbsp sesame seeds
50g/2oz/¹/2 cup hazelnuts, roasted
25g/1oz/¹/4 cup almonds, roughly chopped
50ml/2fl oz/¹/4 cup sunflower oil
50ml/2fl oz/¹/4 cup clear honey
50g/2oz/¹/2 cup raisins
50g/2oz/¹/2 cup dried sweetened
  cranberries
Serves 4

1 Preheat the oven to 140°C/275°F/ Gas 1. Mix together the oats, seeds and nuts in a bowl.

HEALTH BENEFITS

Oats have been the focus of much publicity in recent years; numerous studies have shown that their soluble fibre content can significantly lower blood cholesterol levels. They also supply vitamins B and E, and iron.

2 Heat the oil and honey in a large saucepan until melted, then remove the pan from the heat. Add the oat mixture and stir well. Spread out on one or two baking sheets.

3 Bake for about 50 minutes until crisp, stirring occasionally to prevent the mixture sticking. Remove from the oven and mix in the raisins and cranberries. Leave to cool, then store in an airtight container.

Hot-and-sour Soup

THIS LIGHT AND INVIGORATING soup originates from Thailand. It is best served at the beginning of a Thai meal to stimulate the appetite.

INGREDIENTS

2 carrots

900ml/1 1/2 pints/3 3/4 cups vegetable stock

2 Thai chillies, seeded and finely sliced

2 lemon grass stalks, outer leaves removed and each stalk cut into 3 pieces

4 kaffir lime leaves

2 garlic cloves, finely chopped

4 spring onions, finely sliced

5ml/1 tsp sugar

juice of 1 lime

45ml/3 tbsp chopped fresh coriander

salt

130g/4 1/2oz/1 cup Japanese tofu, sliced

Serves 4

1 To make carrot flowers, cut each carrot in half crossways, then, using a sharp knife, cut four v-shaped channels lengthways. Slice the carrots into thin rounds and set aside.

COOK'S TIP

Kaffir lime leaves have a distinctive citrus flavour. The fresh leaves can be bought from Asian shops, and some supermarkets now sell them dried.

2 Pour the stock into a large saucepan. Reserve 2.5ml/1/2 tsp of the chillies and add the rest to the pan with the lemon grass, lime leaves, garlic and half the spring onions. Bring to the boil, then reduce the heat and simmer for 20 minutes. Strain the stock and discard the flavourings.

3 Return the stock to the pan, add the reserved chillies and spring onions, the sugar, lime juice, coriander and salt to taste.

4 Simmer for 5 minutes, then add the carrot flowers and tofu, and cook for a further 2 minutes until the carrot is just tender. Serve hot.

HEALTH BENEFITS

Hot spices, including chillies, are good for the respiratory system. They help to relieve congestion and may, as a result, soothe the symptoms of colds, flu and hayfever. Chillies encourage the brain to release endorphins, which increase the sensation of pleasure, and so they have been described as aphrodisiacs.

Roasted Root Vegetable Soup

ROASTING THE VEGETABLES GIVES this winter soup a wonderful depth of flavour. You can use other vegetables, if you wish, or adapt the quantities depending on what's in season.

INGREDIENTS

50ml/2fl oz/¼ cup olive oil
1 small butternut squash, peeled, seeded
  and cubed
2 carrots, cut into thick rounds
1 large parsnip, cubed
1 small swede, cubed
2 leeks, thickly sliced
1 onion, quartered
3 bay leaves
4 thyme sprigs, plus extra to garnish
3 rosemary sprigs
1.2 litres/2 pints/5 cups vegetable stock
salt and freshly ground black pepper
soured cream, to serve

Serves 6

1 Preheat the oven to 200°C/400°F/ Gas 6. Put the olive oil into a large bowl. Add the prepared vegetables and toss until coated in the oil.

2 Spread out the vegetables in a single layer on one large or two small baking sheets. Tuck the bay leaves and thyme and rosemary sprigs amongst the vegetables.

COOK'S TIP

Dried herbs can be used in place of fresh; sprinkle 2.5ml/½ tsp of each type over the vegetables in step 2.

3 Roast the vegetables for about 50 minutes until tender, turning them occasionally to make sure they brown evenly. Remove from the oven, discard the herbs and transfer the vegetables to a large saucepan.

HEALTH BENEFITS

This nutritious soup is packed with health-giving vegetables. Butternut squash is particularly high in beta carotene and potassium, which is essential for the functioning of the cells, nerves and muscles. Carrots also contain a high level of beta carotene and are effective detoxifiers.

4 Pour the stock into the pan and bring to the boil. Reduce the heat, season to taste, then simmer for 10 minutes. Transfer the soup to a food processor or blender (or use a hand blender) and process for a few minutes until thick and smooth.

5 Return the soup to the pan to heat through. Season and serve with a swirl of soured cream. Garnish each serving with a sprig of thyme.

Main Dishes

The majority of recipes in this chapter are carbohydrate-based, putting the focus firmly on pulses, such as peas, beans and lentils, and pasta and rice. Not only are these foods filling, they are also packed with fibre, vitamins and minerals, and supply valuable low-fat protein. If this sounds worthy, but not wildly exciting, read on. Included are some of the most innovative vegetarian main course dishes on anybody's menu, from Thai Vegetable Curry with Lemon Grass Rice to Potato, Red Onion and Feta Frittata. Spiced Couscous with Halloumi and Courgette Ribbons is another option, along with Jamaican Black Bean Pot. The emphasis is on interesting ingredients used in imaginative ways. Take a tour of the treats on offer – it's a great way to increase your repertoire of vegetarian dishes and bring new taste sensations to your table.

Main Dishes

Potato, Red Onion and Feta Frittata

THIS ITALIAN OMELETTE IS COOKED
with vegetables and cheese, and is
served flat, like a Spanish tortilla.
Cut it into wedges and serve with
crusty bread and a tomato salad.

INGREDIENTS

25ml/1 1/2 tbsp olive oil
1 red onion, sliced
350g/12oz cooked new potatoes, halved or
    quartered, if large
6 eggs, lightly beaten
115g/4oz/1 cup feta cheese, diced
salt and freshly ground black pepper
Serves 2–4

3 Preheat the grill to high. Season
the beaten eggs, then pour the
mixture over the onion and potatoes.
Sprinkle the cheese on top and cook
over a moderate heat for 5–6 minutes
until the eggs are just set and the base
of the frittata is lightly golden.

4 Place the pan under the
preheated grill (protect the pan
handle with a double layer of foil if it is
not flameproof) and cook the top of
the omelette for about 3 minutes until
it is set and lightly golden. Serve the
frittata warm or cold, cut into wedges.

1 Heat the oil in a large heavy-based,
flameproof frying pan. Add the
onion and sauté for 5 minutes until
softened, stirring occasionally.

2 Add the potatoes and cook for a
further 5 minutes until golden,
stirring to prevent them sticking.
Spread the mixture evenly over the
base of the pan.

HEALTH BENEFITS

*Eggs are an important source of vitamin
B_{12}, which is vital for the nervous system
and the development of red blood cells.
They also supply other B vitamins, zinc
and selenium and a useful amount of
iron. It is beneficial to eat a food rich in
vitamin C at the same time in order to
help the absorption of iron. Do not eat
too many eggs, though – no more than
a maximum of three per week.*

Cheat's Lasagne with Mixed Mushrooms

THIS SIMPLE-TO-ASSEMBLE vegetarian version of lasagne requires neither baking nor the lengthy preparation of various sauces and fillings, but is no less delicious.

INGREDIENTS

40g/1 1/2oz/2/3 cup dried porcini
   mushrooms
50ml/2fl oz/1/4 cup olive oil
1 large garlic clove, chopped
375g/13oz/5 cups mixed mushrooms,
   including brown cap, field, shiitake and
   wild varieties, roughly sliced
175ml/6fl oz/3/4 cup dry white wine
90ml/6 tbsp canned chopped tomatoes
2.5ml/1/2 tsp sugar
8 fresh lasagne sheets
40g/1 1/2oz/1/2 cup freshly grated
   Parmesan cheese
salt and freshly ground black pepper
fresh basil leaves, to garnish

Serves 4

1 Place the porcini mushrooms in a bowl and cover with boiling water. Leave to soak for 15 minutes, then drain and rinse.

2 Heat the olive oil in a large heavy-based frying pan and sauté the soaked mushrooms over a high heat for 5 minutes until the edges are slightly crisp. Reduce the heat, then add the garlic and fresh mushrooms, and sauté for a further 5 minutes until tender, stirring occasionally.

3 Add the wine and cook for 5–7 minutes until reduced. Stir in the tomatoes, sugar and seasoning and cook over a medium heat for about 5 minutes until thickened.

4 Meanwhile, cook the lasagne according to the instructions on the packet until it is *al dente*. Drain lightly – the pasta should still be moist.

5 To serve, spoon a little of the sauce on to each of four warm serving plates. Place a sheet of lasagne on top and spoon a quarter of the mushroom sauce over each serving. Sprinkle with some Parmesan and top with another pasta sheet. Sprinkle with black pepper and more Parmesan and garnish with basil leaves.

HEALTH BENEFITS

Shiitake mushrooms, a valuable source of zinc, iron and potassium, are reputed to help thin the blood and consequently to reduce the risk of heart disease.

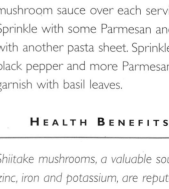

Tomato and Lentil Dahl with Toasted Almonds

RICHLY FLAVOURED WITH spices, coconut milk and tomatoes, this lentil dish makes a filling supper. Warm naan bread and natural yogurt are all that are needed as accompaniments. Split red lentils give the dish a vibrant colour, but you could use larger yellow split peas instead, if you wish.

INGREDIENTS

30ml/2 tbsp vegetable oil
1 large onion, finely chopped
3 garlic cloves, chopped
1 carrot, diced
10ml/2 tsp cumin seeds
10ml/2 tsp yellow mustard seeds
2.5cm/1in piece fresh root ginger, grated
10ml/2 tsp ground turmeric
5ml/1 tsp mild chilli powder
5ml/1 tsp garam masala
225g/8oz/1 cup split red lentils
400ml/14fl oz/1²/3 cups water
400ml/14fl oz/1²/3 cups coconut milk
5 tomatoes, peeled, seeded and chopped
juice of 2 limes
60ml/4 tbsp chopped fresh coriander
salt and freshly ground black pepper
25g/1oz/1/4 cup flaked almonds, toasted,
   to serve
Serves 4

HEALTH BENEFITS

• Spices have long been recognized for their medicinal qualities, from curing flatulence (useful when added to a pulse dish) to warding off colds and flu.
• Lentils are a useful source of low-fat protein. They contain good amounts of B vitamins and provide a rich source of zinc and iron.
• You need to eat foods rich in vitamin C at the same meal to improve absorption of iron. Limes are a good source, but you could also serve a fresh fruit dessert containing apples, kiwi fruit and oranges.

1 Heat the oil in a large heavy-based saucepan. Sauté the onion for 5 minutes until softened, stirring occasionally. Add the garlic, carrot, cumin and mustard seeds, and ginger. Cook for 5 minutes, stirring, until the seeds begin to pop and the carrot softens slightly.

2 Stir in the ground turmeric, chilli powder and garam masala, and cook for 1 minute or until the flavours begin to mingle, stirring to prevent the spices burning.

3 Add the lentils, water, coconut milk and tomatoes, and season well. Bring to the boil, then reduce the heat and simmer, covered for about 45 minutes, stirring occasionally to prevent the lentils sticking.

4 Stir in the lime juice and 45ml/ 3 tbsp of the fresh coriander, then check the seasoning. Cook for a further 15 minutes until the lentils soften and become tender. To serve, sprinkle with the remaining coriander and the flaked almonds.

Mushroom, Nut and Prune Jalousie

JALOUSIE, THE FRENCH WORD for shutter, refers to this pie's slatted top. The pie has a rich, nutty filling and, served with crisp roast potatoes and steamed vegetables, makes a great alternative to the Sunday joint.

INGREDIENTS

75g/3oz/1/3 cup green lentils, rinsed
5ml/1 tsp vegetable bouillon powder
15ml/1 tbsp sunflower oil
2 large leeks, sliced
2 garlic cloves, chopped
200g/7oz/3 cups field mushrooms,
    finely chopped
10ml/2 tsp dried mixed herbs
75g/3oz/3/4 cup chopped mixed nuts
15ml/1 tbsp pine nuts (optional)
75g/3oz/1/3 cup ready-to-eat pitted prunes
25g/1oz/1/2 cup fresh breadcrumbs
2 eggs, beaten
2 sheets ready-rolled puff pastry, total
    weight about 425g/15oz
flour, for dusting
salt and freshly ground black pepper
Serves 6

1 Put the lentils in a saucepan and cover with cold water. Bring to the boil, then reduce the heat and add the vegetable bouillon powder. Partly cover the pan and simmer for 20 minutes or until the lentils are tender. Set aside.

2 Heat the oil in a large heavy-based frying pan, add the leeks and garlic and fry for 5 minutes or until softened. Add the mushrooms and herbs and cook for a further 5 minutes. Transfer the mushroom mixture to a bowl using a slotted spoon. Stir in the nuts, pine nuts, if using, prunes, breadcrumbs and lentils.

COOK'S TIP

Try other combinations of vegetables, nuts and dried fruit.

3 Preheat the oven to 220°C/425°F/Gas 7. Add two-thirds of the beaten egg to the mushroom mixture and season well. Set aside and leave to cool.

4 Meanwhile, unroll one of the pastry sheets. Cut off 2.5cm/1in from its width and length, then lay it on a dampened baking sheet. Unroll the second pastry sheet, dust lightly with flour, then fold in half lengthways. Make a series of cuts across the fold, 1cm/1/2in apart, leaving a 2.5cm/1in border around the edge of the pastry.

5 Spoon the mushroom mixture evenly over the pastry base, leaving a 2.5cm/1in border. Dampen the edges of the pastry with water. Open out the folded piece of pastry and carefully lay it over the top of the filling. Trim the edges, if necessary, then press the edges of the pastry together to seal and crimp the edges.

6 Brush the top of the pastry with the remaining beaten egg and bake for 25–30 minutes until golden. Leave to cool slightly before serving.

Layered Polenta Bake

POLENTA, TOMATOES, SPINACH and beans make a tasty supper dish.

INGREDIENTS
5ml/1 tsp salt
375g/13oz/3 cups fine polenta
olive oil, for greasing and brushing
25g/1oz/⅓ cup freshly grated
   Parmesan cheese
salt and freshly ground black pepper

For the tomato sauce
15ml/1 tbsp olive oil
2 garlic cloves, chopped
400g/14oz/3 cups chopped tomatoes
15ml/1 tbsp chopped fresh sage
2.5ml/½ tsp soft brown sugar
200g/7oz/1½ cups canned cannellini
   beans, rinsed and drained

For the spinach sauce
250g/9oz spinach, tough stalks removed
150ml/¼ pint/⅔ cup single cream
115g/4oz/1 cup Gorgonzola cheese, cubed
large pinch of ground nutmeg
Serves 6

1 Make the polenta. Bring 2 litres/ 3½ pints/8 cups water to the boil in a large heavy-based saucepan and add the salt. Remove the pan from the heat. Gradually pour in the polenta, whisking continuously.

2 Return the pan to the heat and stir constantly for 15–20 minutes until the polenta is thick and comes away from the side of the pan. Remove the pan from the heat.

3 Season well with pepper, then spoon the polenta on to a wet work surface or piece of marble. Using a wet spatula, spread out the polenta until it is 1cm/½in thick. Leave to cool for about 1 hour.

4 Preheat the oven to 190°C/ 375°F/Gas 5. To make the tomato sauce, heat the oil in a saucepan, then fry the garlic for 1 minute. Add the tomatoes and sage and bring to the boil. Reduce the heat, add the sugar and seasoning, and simmer for 10 minutes until slightly reduced, stirring occasionally. Stir in the beans and cook for a further 2 minutes.

5 Meanwhile, wash the spinach thoroughly and place in a large pan with only the water that clings to the leaves. Cover the pan tightly and cook over a medium heat for about 3 minutes or until tender, stirring occasionally. Tip the spinach into a colander and drain, then squeeze out as much excess water as possible with the back of a wooden spoon.

6 Heat the cream, cheese and nutmeg in a small heavy-based saucepan. Bring to the boil, then reduce the heat. Stir in the spinach and seasoning, then cook gently until slightly thickened, stirring frequently.

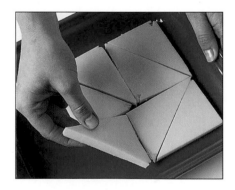

7 Cut the polenta into triangles, then place a layer of polenta in an oiled deep baking dish. Spoon over the tomato sauce, then top with another layer of polenta. Top with the spinach sauce and cover with the remaining polenta triangles. Brush with olive oil, sprinkle with Parmesan and bake for 35–40 minutes. Heat the grill to high and grill until the top is golden before serving.

Chestnut, Stilton and Ale Pie

THIS HEARTY WINTER DISH has a rich Guinness gravy and a herb pastry top. The Stilton adds a delicious creaminess but can be left out to make a less rich version of the pie.

INGREDIENTS

30ml/2 tbsp sunflower oil
2 large onions, chopped
500g/1¼lb/8 cups button
  mushrooms, halved
3 carrots, sliced
1 parsnip, cut into thick slices
15ml/1 tbsp fresh thyme or 5ml/1 tsp dried
2 bay leaves
250ml/8fl oz/1 cup Guinness
120ml/4fl oz/½ cup vegetable stock
5ml/1 tsp vegetarian Worcestershire sauce
5ml/1 tsp soft dark brown sugar
350g/12oz/3 cups canned chestnuts,
  halved
30ml/2 tbsp unbleached plain flour
150g/5oz/1¼ cups Stilton cheese, cubed
1 egg, beaten, or milk, to glaze
salt and freshly ground black pepper

For the pastry
115g/4oz/1 cup wholemeal flour
a pinch of salt
50g/2oz/4 tbsp unsalted butter or
  vegetable margarine
15ml/1 tbsp fresh thyme or 5ml/1 tsp dried
Serves 4

1 To make the pastry, rub together the flour, salt and butter or margarine until the mixture resembles fine breadcrumbs. Add the thyme and enough water to form a soft dough.

HEALTH BENEFITS

Chestnuts contain useful amounts of B complex vitamins, potassium and calcium and, unlike other nuts, they are very low in fat.

2 Turn out the dough on to a floured board or work surface and gently knead for 1 minute until it forms a smooth dough. Wrap in clear film and chill for 30 minutes.

3 Meanwhile, to make the filling, heat the oil in a heavy-based saucepan and fry the onions for 5 minutes until softened, stirring occasionally. Add the mushrooms and cook for a further 3 minutes or until just tender. Add the carrots, parsnip and herbs, stir and cover the pan. Cook for 3 minutes until slightly softened.

4 Pour in the Guinness, vegetable stock and Worcestershire sauce, then add the sugar and seasoning. Simmer, covered, for 5 minutes, stirring occasionally. Add the chestnuts.

5 Mix the flour to a paste with 30ml/ 2 tbsp water. Add to the Guinness mixture and cook, uncovered, for 5 minutes until the sauce thickens, stirring. Stir in the cheese and heat until melted, stirring constantly.

6 Preheat the oven to 220°C/ 425°F/Gas 7. Roll out the pastry to fit the top of a 1.5 litre/2½ pint/ 6¼ cup deep pie dish. Spoon the chestnut mixture into the dish. Dampen the edges of the dish and cover with the pastry. Seal, trim and crimp the edges. Cut a small slit in the top of the pie and use any surplus pastry to make pastry leaves. Brush with egg or milk and bake for 30 minutes until the pastry is golden.

Avocado, Red Onion and Spinach Salad with Polenta Croûtons

THE SIMPLE LEMON DRESSING gives a sharp tang to creamy avocado, sweet red onions and crisp spinach. Golden polenta croûtons, with their crunchy golden exterior and soft centre, add a delicious contrast.

INGREDIENTS

1 large red onion, cut into wedges
300g/11oz ready-made polenta, cut into
    1cm/1/2in cubes
olive oil, for brushing
225g/8oz baby spinach leaves
1 avocado, peeled, stoned and sliced
5ml/1 tsp lemon juice

For the dressing
60ml/4 tbsp extra virgin olive oil
juice of 1/2 lemon
salt and freshly ground black pepper
Serves 4

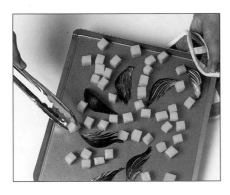

1 Preheat the oven to 200°C/400°F/ Gas 6. Place the onion wedges and polenta cubes on a lightly oiled baking sheet and bake for 25 minutes or until the onion is tender and the polenta is crisp and golden, turning them regularly to prevent them sticking. Leave to cool slightly.

2 Meanwhile, make the dressing. Place the olive oil, lemon juice and seasoning to taste in a bowl or screw-top jar. Stir or shake thoroughly to combine.

3 Place the baby spinach leaves in a serving bowl. Toss the avocado slices in the lemon juice to prevent them browning, then add to the spinach with the roasted onions.

4 Pour the dressing over the salad and toss gently to combine. Sprinkle the polenta croûtons on top or hand them round separately and serve immediately.

HEALTH BENEFITS

Avocados have been traditionally regarded as a high fat food that should be avoided. However, although they do contain high amounts of fat, it is beneficial monounsaturated fat, and new research has revealed that regularly eating avocados can actually decrease the level of cholesterol in the body. Avocados also have a valuable mineral content and eating them can improve the condition of your skin and hair.

COOK'S TIP

If you can't find ready-made polenta, you can make your own using instant polenta grains. Simply cook according to the packet instructions, then pour into a tray and leave to cool and set.

Roasted Tomato and Mozzarella Salad with Basil Dressing

ROASTING THE TOMATOES adds a new dimension to this salad. Make the basil oil just before serving to retain its fresh flavour and vivid colour.

INGREDIENTS

6 large plum tomatoes
olive oil, for brushing
2 balls fresh mozzarella cheese, cut into
   8–12 slices
salt and freshly ground black pepper
basil leaves, to garnish

For the basil oil
25 basil leaves
60ml/4 tbsp extra virgin olive oil
1 garlic clove, crushed
Serves 4

1 Preheat the oven to 200°C/400°F/ Gas 6 and oil a baking tray. Cut the tomatoes in half lengthways and remove the seeds. Place skin-side down on the baking tray and roast for 20 minutes or until the tomatoes are tender but still retain their shape.

2 Meanwhile, make the basil oil. Place the basil leaves, olive oil and garlic in a food processor or blender and process until smooth. Transfer to a bowl and chill until required.

3 For each serving, place the tomato halves on top of 2 or 3 slices of mozzarella and drizzle over the oil. Season well. Garnish with basil leaves and serve at once.

HEALTH BENEFITS

Basil is a natural tranquillizer and calms the nervous system. It can also stimulate the appetite and is good for the digestion, easing cramps and nausea.

Mixed Herb Salad with Toasted Mixed Seeds

THIS SIMPLE SALAD is the perfect antidote to a rich, heavy meal as it contains fresh herbs that can ease the digestion. Balsamic vinegar adds a rich, sweet taste to the dressing, but red or white wine vinegar could be used instead.

INGREDIENTS

90g/3¹/₂oz/4 cups mixed salad leaves
50g/2oz/2 cups mixed salad herbs, such as
   coriander, parsley, basil and rocket
25g/1oz/3 tbsp pumpkin seeds
25g/1oz/3 tbsp sunflower seeds

For the dressing
60ml/4 tbsp extra virgin olive oil
15ml/1 tbsp balsamic vinegar
2.5 ml/¹/₂ tsp Dijon mustard
salt and freshly ground black pepper
Serves 4

1 To make the dressing, combine the ingredients in a bowl or screw-top jar, shake or mix with a small whisk or fork until combined.

HEALTH BENEFITS

• *Parsley contains useful amounts of vitamin C and iron.*
• *Pumpkin and sunflower seeds, although high in calories, are full of useful vitamins, minerals and fibre, including iron, vitamin E and zinc.*

2 Put the salad and herb leaves in a large bowl.

3 Toast the pumpkin and sunflower seeds in a dry frying pan over a medium heat for 2 minutes until golden, tossing frequently to prevent them burning. Allow the seeds to cool slightly before sprinkling them over the salad.

4 Pour the dressing over the salad and toss with your hands until the leaves are well coated, then serve.

Feta and Mint Potato Salad

FETA CHEESE, YOGURT AND fresh mint combine perfectly with warm new potatoes in this salad.

INGREDIENTS

500g/1¼lb pink fir apple potatoes
90g/3½oz feta cheese, crumbled

For the dressing
225g/8oz/1 cup natural live yogurt
15g/½oz/½ cup fresh mint leaves
30ml/2 tbsp mayonnaise
salt and freshly ground black pepper
Serves 4

COOK'S TIPS

Pink fir apple potatoes have a smooth waxy texture and retain their shape when cooked, making them ideal for salads. Charlotte and other special salad potatoes could be used instead.

1 Steam the potatoes over a pan of boiling water for about 20 minutes until tender, then drain well and tip into a large bowl.

HEALTH BENEFITS

Potatoes are often considered to be fattening, but it is usually the method of preparation that is to be blamed. Steaming adds no calories and preserves the vitamin C content.

2 Meanwhile, make the dressing. Place the yogurt and mint in a food processor for a few minutes until the mint leaves are finely chopped. Transfer the dressing to a small bowl.

3 Stir in the mayonnaise and season to taste. Spoon the dressing over the warm potatoes and scatter with the feta cheese. Serve immediately.

Apple and Beetroot Salad with Red Leaves

BITTER LEAVES ARE COMPLEMENTED by sweet-flavoured apples and beetroot in this summer salad.

INGREDIENTS

50g/2oz/⅓ cup whole unblanched almonds
2 red apples, cored and diced
juice of ½ lemon
115g/4oz/4 cups red salad leaves, such as lollo rosso, oak leaf and radicchio
200g/7oz cooked beetroot in natural juice, sliced

For the dressing
30ml/2 tbsp olive oil
15ml/1 tbsp walnut oil
15ml/1 tbsp red or white wine vinegar
salt and freshly ground black pepper
Serves 4

1 Toast the almonds in a dry frying pan for 2–3 minutes until golden brown, tossing frequently to prevent them burning.

2 Meanwhile, make the dressing. Put the olive and walnut oils, vinegar and seasoning in a bowl or screw-top jar. Stir or shake thoroughly to combine.

3 Toss the apples in lemon juice to prevent them browning, then place in a large bowl and add the salad leaves, beetroot and almonds. Pour over the dressing and toss gently.

HEALTH BENEFITS

Red fruits and vegetables have high levels of vitamins C and E and beta carotene.

Split Pea and Shallot Mash

GREATLY UNDERRATED, SPLIT PEAS are delicious when puréed with shallots and enlivened with cumin seeds and fresh herbs. The purée makes an excellent alternative to mashed potatoes, and is particularly good with winter pies and nut roasts. It can also be served with warmed pitta bread, accompanied by diced tomatoes and a splash of olive oil.

INGREDIENTS

225g/8oz/1 cup yellow split peas
1 bay leaf
8 sage leaves, roughly chopped
15ml/1 tbsp olive oil
3 shallots, finely chopped
8ml/heaped 1 tsp cumin seeds
1 large garlic clove, chopped
50g/2oz/4 tbsp butter, softened
salt and freshly ground black pepper
Serves 4–6

1 Place the split peas in a bowl and cover with cold water. Leave to soak overnight, then rinse and drain.

2 Place the peas in a saucepan, cover with fresh cold water and bring to the boil. Skim off any foam that rises to the surface, then reduce the heat. Add the bay leaf and sage, and simmer for 30–40 minutes until the peas are tender. Add more water during cooking, if necessary.

3 Meanwhile, heat the oil in a frying pan and cook the shallots, cumin seeds and garlic for 3 minutes or until the shallots soften, stirring occasionally. Add the mixture to the split peas while they are still cooking.

4 Drain the split peas, reserving the cooking water. Remove the bay leaf, then place the split peas in a food processor or blender with the butter and season well.

5 Add 105ml/7 tbsp of the reserved cooking water and blend until the mixture forms a coarse purée. Add more water if the mash seems to be too dry. Adjust the seasoning and serve warm.

HEALTH BENEFITS

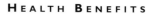

Split peas, like other pulses, are an excellent source of protein, fibre, minerals and B vitamins. They are particularly good for diabetics as they can help to control blood sugar levels.

Root Vegetable Gratin with Indian Spices

SUBTLY SPICED WITH CURRY powder, turmeric, coriander and mild chilli powder, this rich gratin is substantial enough to serve on its own for lunch or supper. It also makes a good accompaniment to a vegetable or bean curry.

INGREDIENTS

2 large potatoes, total weight about 450g/1lb

2 sweet potatoes, total weight about 275g/10oz

175g/6oz celeriac

15ml/1 tbsp unsalted butter

5ml/1 tsp curry powder

5ml/1 tsp ground turmeric

2.5ml/^{1}/2 tsp ground coriander

5ml/1 tsp mild chilli powder

3 shallots, chopped

salt and freshly ground black pepper

150ml/^{1}/4 pint/^{2}/3 cup single cream

150ml/^{1}/4 pint/^{2}/3 cup semi-skimmed milk

chopped fresh flat leaf parsley, to garnish

Serves 4

1 Thinly slice the potatoes, sweet potatoes and celeriac, using a sharp knife or the slicing attachment on a food processor. Immediately place the vegetables in a bowl of cold water to prevent them discolouring.

COOK'S TIP

The cream adds richness to this gratin; use semi-skimmed milk, if you prefer.

2 Preheat the oven to 180°C/ 350°F/Gas 4. Heat half the butter in a heavy-based saucepan, add the curry powder, turmeric and coriander and half the chilli powder. Cook for 2 minutes, then leave to cool slightly. Drain the vegetables, then pat dry with kitchen paper. Place in a bowl, add the spice mixture and the shallots and mix well.

HEALTH BENEFITS

This gratin contains ground spices, which boost a sluggish digestion and have a beneficial effect on the circulation.

3 Arrange the vegetables in a gratin dish, seasoning between the layers. Mix together the cream and milk, pour the mixture over the vegetables, then sprinkle the remaining chilli powder on top.

4 Cover with greaseproof paper and bake for about 45 minutes. Remove the greaseproof paper, dot with the remaining butter and bake for a further 50 minutes until the top is golden. Serve garnished with chopped fresh parsley.

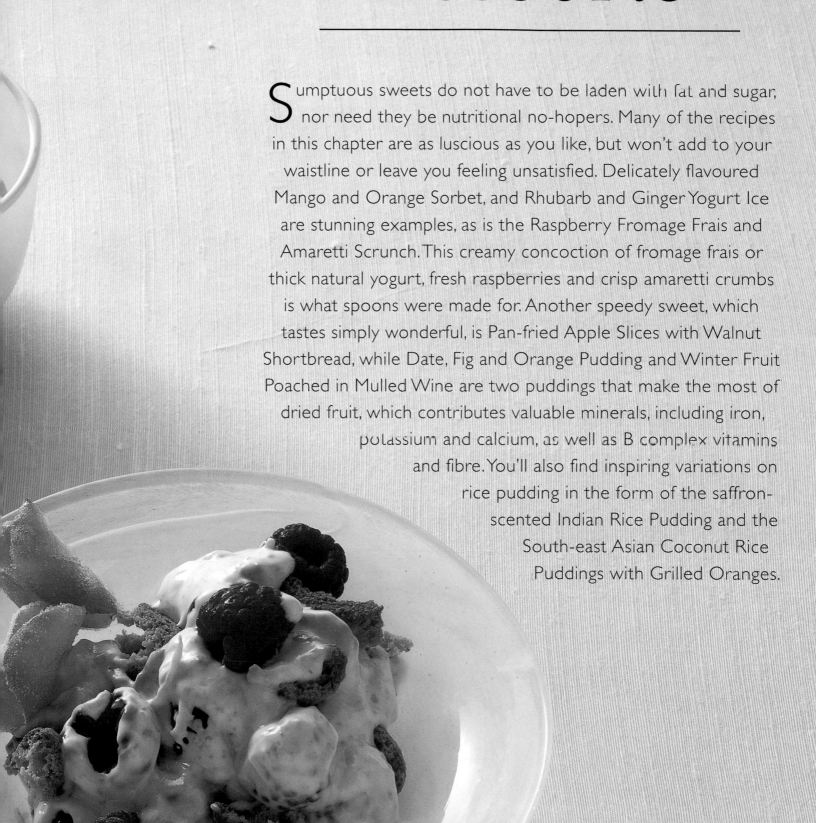

Desserts

Sumptuous sweets do not have to be laden with fat and sugar, nor need they be nutritional no-hopers. Many of the recipes in this chapter are as luscious as you like, but won't add to your waistline or leave you feeling unsatisfied. Delicately flavoured Mango and Orange Sorbet, and Rhubarb and Ginger Yogurt Ice are stunning examples, as is the Raspberry Fromage Frais and Amaretti Scrunch. This creamy concoction of fromage frais or thick natural yogurt, fresh raspberries and crisp amaretti crumbs is what spoons were made for. Another speedy sweet, which tastes simply wonderful, is Pan-fried Apple Slices with Walnut Shortbread, while Date, Fig and Orange Pudding and Winter Fruit Poached in Mulled Wine are two puddings that make the most of dried fruit, which contributes valuable minerals, including iron, potassium and calcium, as well as B complex vitamins and fibre. You'll also find inspiring variations on rice pudding in the form of the saffron-scented Indian Rice Pudding and the South-east Asian Coconut Rice Puddings with Grilled Oranges.

Mango and Orange Sorbet

FRESH AND TANGY, AND gloriously vibrant in colour, this sorbet is the perfect finale for a spicy meal.

INGREDIENTS

115g/4oz/½ cup golden caster sugar
2 large mangoes
juice of 1 orange
1 egg white (optional)
thinly pared strips of fresh unwaxed orange
    rind, to decorate

Serves 2–4

1 Gently heat the sugar and 300ml/½ pint/1¼ cups water in a pan until the sugar has dissolved. Bring to the boil, then reduce the heat and simmer for 5 minutes. Leave to cool.

2 Cut away the two sides of the mango close to the stone. Peel, then cut the flesh from the stone. Dice the fruit and discard the stone.

3 Process the mango flesh and orange juice in a food processor with the sugar syrup until smooth.

4 Pour the mixture into a freezer-proof container and freeze for 2 hours until semi-frozen. Whisk the egg white, if using, until it forms stiff peaks, then stir it into the sorbet. Whisk well to remove any ice crystals and freeze until solid.

5 Transfer the sorbet to the fridge 10 minutes before serving. Serve, decorated with orange rind.

HEALTH BENEFITS

Mangoes and oranges aid the digestion, boost the immune system and are said to cleanse the blood. They are also an excellent source of vitamins C and A.

Rhubarb and Ginger Yogurt Ice

THIS DELICATE PINK YOGURT ice is flavoured with honey and ginger.

INGREDIENTS

300g/11oz/scant 1½ cups set natural
    live yogurt
200g/7oz/scant 1 cup fromage frais
375g/13oz/3 cups rhubarb, trimmed
    and chopped
45ml/3 tbsp stem ginger syrup
30ml/2 tbsp clear honey
3 pieces stem ginger, finely chopped

Serves 6

1 In a bowl, whisk together the yogurt and fromage frais.

2 Pour the yogurt mixture into a shallow freezer-proof container and freeze for 1 hour.

3 Meanwhile, put the rhubarb, stem ginger syrup and honey in a large saucepan and cook over a low heat for 15 minutes, or until the rhubarb is soft. Leave to cool, then purée in a food processor or blender.

4 Remove the semi-frozen yogurt mixture from the freezer and fold in the rhubarb and stem ginger purée. Beat well until smooth. Add the chopped stem ginger.

5 Return the yogurt ice to the freezer and freeze for a further 2 hours. Remove from the freezer and beat again, then freeze until solid. Serve scoops of the yogurt ice on individual plates or in bowls.

HEALTH BENEFITS

• Rhubarb is rich in potassium and is an effective laxative. However, it is also high in oxalic acid, which is reputed to inhibit the absorption of iron and calcium and can exasperate joint problems, such as arthritis. The leaves are poisonous and should never be eaten.
• Stem ginger retains many of the health-giving qualities of fresh ginger. It aids digestion and is effective in treating gastrointestinal disorders.

COOK'S TIP

Take the yogurt ice out of the freezer and transfer it to the fridge 15 minutes before serving to allow it to soften.

Winter Fruit Poached in Mulled Wine

FRESH APPLES AND PEARS ARE combined with dried apricots and figs, and cooked in a fragrant, spicy wine until tender and intensely flavoured.

INGREDIENTS

300ml/½ pint/1¼ cups red wine
300ml/½ pint/1¼ cups fresh orange juice
finely grated rind and juice of 1 orange
45ml/3 tbsp clear honey or barley
   malt syrup
1 cinnamon stick, broken in half
4 cloves
4 cardamom pods, split
2 pears, such as Comice or William, peeled,
   cored and halved
8 ready-to-eat dried figs
12 ready-to-eat dried unsulphured apricots
2 eating apples, peeled, cored and
   thickly sliced

Serves 4

1 Put the wine, the fresh and squeezed orange juice and half the orange rind in a saucepan with the honey or syrup and spices. Bring to the boil, then reduce the heat and simmer for 2 minutes, stirring occasionally.

HEALTH BENEFITS

• *The combination of fresh and dried fruit ensures a healthy amount of vitamins and minerals, particularly vitamins C, beta carotene, potassium and iron. The fruit is also rich in fibre.*

• *Cardamom and cinnamon soothe indigestion and, along with cloves, can offer relief from colds and coughs.*

2 Add the pears, figs and apricots to the pan and cook, covered, for 25 minutes, occasionally turning the fruit in the wine mixture. Add the sliced apples and cook for a further 12–15 minutes until the fruit is tender.

3 Remove the fruit from the pan and discard the spices. Cook the wine mixture over a high heat until reduced and syrupy, then pour it over the fruit. Serve decorated with the reserved strips of orange rind, if wished.

Fruit Soda Bread

THIS TRADITIONAL IRISH BREAD IS quick to make as it does not require prolonged kneading or rising. It is best eaten while still warm on the day of baking.

INGREDIENTS

225g/8oz/2 cups unbleached plain flour
225g/8oz/2 cups wholemeal flour
5ml/1 tsp salt
5ml/1 tsp bicarbonate of soda
20ml/heaped 1 tbsp sugar
75g/3oz/3/4 cup raisins
50g/2oz/1/4 cup ready-to-eat stoned
   prunes, chopped
1 egg, lightly beaten
300ml/1/2 pint/1 1/4 cups buttermilk
Serves 4

1 Preheat the oven to 200°C/400°F/ Gas 6. Sift together the plain and wholemeal flours, salt and bicarbonate of soda into a large bowl, adding any bran left in the sieve. Add the sugar and dried fruit, and mix well to combine.

2 Make a well in the centre and add the egg and buttermilk. Mix first with a wooden spoon and then with your hands until it forms a soft, slightly sticky dough. If the dough is too dry, add a little more buttermilk.

HEALTH BENEFITS

Dried fruit is recognized as a good source of fibre as well as minerals, such as potassium and iron.

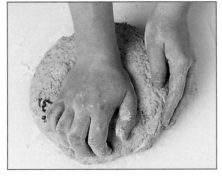

3 Turn out the dough on to a lightly floured work surface and knead lightly until smooth. Form into a flat round, about 4cm/1 1/2in thick.

4 Place on a greased baking sheet and dust the loaf with plain flour.

5 Cut a large deep cross, almost through to the bottom of the dough round. Bake for 30–35 minutes until risen and golden. The bread should sound hollow when tapped underneath. Transfer to a wire rack and leave to cool.

Rosemary and Rock Salt Focaccia

ENRICHED WITH OLIVE OIL and flavoured with rosemary, garlic and black olives, this popular Italian bread takes its name from the Italian word for hearth – which is where it was traditionally baked.

INGREDIENTS

225g/8oz/2 cups unbleached plain
   flour, sifted
2.5ml/1/2 tsp salt
7g/1/4oz sachet easy-blend dried yeast
4 garlic cloves, finely chopped
2 sprigs of rosemary, leaves removed
   and chopped
10 black olives, stoned and roughly
   chopped (optional)
15ml/1 tbsp olive oil

For the topping
90ml/6 tbsp olive oil
10ml/2 tsp rock salt
1 sprig of rosemary, leaves removed
Makes 1 loaf

1 Mix together the flour, salt, yeast, garlic, rosemary and olives, if using, in a large bowl. Make a well in the centre and add the olive oil and 150ml/1/4 pint/2/3 cup warm water. Mix thoroughly to form a soft dough.

HEALTH BENEFITS

The oil in olives is monounsaturated and this type of oil is believed to reduce blood cholesterol levels. Olives also provide good amounts of iron and the antioxidant, vitamin E.

2 Turn out the dough on to a floured work surface and knead for 10–15 minutes. Put the dough in an oiled bowl and cover with oiled clear film or a dish towel. Leave to rise in a warm place for 45 minutes, until the dough has doubled in bulk.

3 Turn out the dough and knead lightly again. Roll out to an oval shape, about 1cm/1/2in thick.

4 Place the dough on a greased baking sheet, cover loosely with oiled clear film or a dish towel and leave in a warm place for 25–30 minutes to rise again.

5 Preheat the oven to 200°C/ 400°F/Gas 6. Make indentations with your fingertips all over the top of the bread. Drizzle two-thirds of the olive oil over the top, then sprinkle with the rock salt and rosemary. Bake for 25 minutes until golden.

6 When ready, the bread will sound hollow when tapped underneath. Transfer to a wire rack and spoon the remaining olive oil over the top.

VARIATIONS

• *To make sun-dried tomato focaccia, omit the rosemary leaves and olives, and add 75g/3oz/11/2 cups chopped and drained sun-dried tomatoes in oil to the dry ingredients. Add 15ml/1 tbsp sun-dried tomato purée and 15ml/1 tbsp of the oil from the sun-dried tomatoes to the dough when adding the oil and water, then mix well.*
• *To make saffron focaccia, add a few strands of saffron to the warm water and leave to stand for 5 minutes before adding to the flour. Alternatively, add a pinch of saffron powder to the flour.*